SENSELESS: THE ANDRE ADEREMI STORY

A MOTHERS MEMOIR

Yemi Hughes

This book is a memoir. It reflects the author's present recollections of experiences over time. Some names and characteristics have been changed to protect some of the lovely people that were part of the author's life during the events she has written about, some events have been compressed, and some dialogue has been recreated.

Some names remain the same because those people have either agreed to have their identity included, and some who have not agreed could be identified by a simple internet search about events at the time. Quite frankly, some of them don't deserve to have their identities protected either.

The author has tried to be as factual as possible and restrict her emotions and opinions so as not to offend, but this has not always been possible.

CHAPTER 1 – INTRODUCTION

CHAPTER 2 – THE SHOOTING

CHAPTER 3 – CRIMINAL DAMAGE

CHAPTER 4– DRIVE-BY SHOOTING

CHAPTER 5 – A LONG WAY FROM HOME

CHAPTER 6– 16TH AUGUST PART 1

CHAPTER 7 – 16TH AUGUST PART 2

CHAPTER 8 – THE MORNING AFTER THE NIGHT BEFORE

CHAPTER 9 – INVESTIGATIONS AND ARRESTS

CHAPTER 10 – PICKING UP THE PIECES

CHAPTER 11 – PLANNING THE FUNERAL

CHAPTER 12 – ANDRE'S FINAL FAREWELL

CHAPTER 13 – THE ESCAPE

CHAPTER 14 – THE TRIAL WITNESSES AND EVIDENCE

CHAPTER 15 – THE TRIAL DEFENDANT'S FAMILIES

CHAPTER 16 – THE TRIAL VERDICTS AND SENTENCING

CHAPTER 17 – THE DAY AFTER

CHAPTER 18 – ONE YEAR MEMORIAL

CHAPTER 19 – LIVING WITHOUT HIM AND REFLECTIONS

CHAPTER 1
INTRODUCTION

I have been writing this book for over two years; the reason I started I am now unsure of because there have been so many changes in my life since I first put my thoughts and feelings onto paper. I was sure I needed to create a long-lasting legacy for my beautiful son Andre that would last long after even I leave this world. Throughout the time that I have been writing, I have undertaken Trauma therapy to help me cope with the overwhelming grief that comes with losing a child. Nobody but those who have had a child taken away by murder can understand the emotional torment that murder can cause in your life, even more so if it is your child that has been snatched out of the world prematurely. Death in this way is a tragedy. I have only ever lost loved ones through illness or old age, and although grief still exists, those times have been, on reflection, more emotionally manageable than what I went through when I heard that my son was dead.

What I hoped to achieve from writing was to share a bit of who Andre was. For me, it was important that anyone who read this book could get a real sense of his personality and what he contributed to the world, in his short number of years. All mothers love their children whether they do right in the eyes of society or not. A special bond between these two people, mother, and child, is undeniable. We don't always like the things they do or the ways that they behave, but when it comes down to the nuts and bolts of it, they belong to us; we made them, we carried them inside our bodies and eventually birthed them into the world. If that doesn't create something special between two people, then I don't know what else can.

I believe if I had written this book earlier in my healing journey, it would have been a very different account. Although the version of events would have remained the same, the emotion I put forth would have been different. It has taken almost six years for me to get to a place where I can talk about the events of 16th August without feeling anger. Anger consumes people, and I found myself on a journey that was taking me nowhere but down. I had to make peace with my demons and dig deep inside to be at the place of peace I am now in. That wasn't easy. I had to fight. I spent so long in a dark place that everyone could visibly see. I was underground, and there was no exit. From that place, I made the conscious decision that I needed to heal, to get better mentally and physically. I spent a long time gliding along like a swan on top of the water whilst underneath; I was paddling so hard to keep my head above the dark place I was in. I have forced myself to face everything head on; not originally for myself, but for my children. You will read how I had to remove toxic habits from my life, including friends, to start moving upwards.

Throughout this time, I kept most of my feelings from my family and friends, and this was when I started to engage in all things Youth Violence. I had to stay busy and keep my son alive in mine and everyone else's memories. I threw myself at any opportunity and engaged myself in a plight to rid the community of knife crime. Why wasn't Andre's murder enough for the young people to commit to putting down their weapons and live in peace? Andre became one of many that I watched fall at a young age. I became obsessed with the fight to change the world. I attended knife crime rallies, spoke to Police, and talked to the young people in the hope of getting them to reflect and I also campaigned to raise money for bleed control kits; inspired by another bereaved mother, to at least offer some solution to keeping young people alive on our streets if they were stabbed. I dedicated many years of my life after losing Andre to the cause and have met many people along the way who have been on the same journey. My proudest moments during this time which don't feature in this book, are appearing on the special episode of Eastender, being invited to watch 42nd street by Bonnie Langford and having the opportunity to go backstage and meet with her after the performance.

Bonnie watched me sob on set at her on-screen son's funeral. The sight of someone else walking behind a coffin whilst crying triggered me. It was a strange feeling because even though I knew it wasn't real, I expressed all the emotions on that day that I hadn't on Andre's day. Bonnie noticed me wiping away the tears with what must have been a look of horror on my face and came over to hug me. I explained to her that I felt silly because I hadn't even cried at my son's funeral, but I understand that now, I know exactly why I held everything back. I had to be in control and showing signs of heartbreak and grief on that day; I couldn't do.

I feel that I have been running a race. There are other mothers in the race too, and although we are all fighting for the same thing, which stops other mothers from having to join the race, sometimes it does feel like a race that is going anywhere. The competition is real. I don't want to compete with anyone, and sometimes the reality of other people's grief makes them react to situations in ways that I sometimes don't understand, and it often knocks the wind out of my sails. Everything that I have tried to do has been with the best intention, and just like all the others who have to continue living in this upside-down world without their loved ones, we continue to keep our children's names alive. Unfortunately, sometimes this comes at the expense of others. The sad reality is that nobody who has lost their life, including my Andre, is more important than anyone else who has lost their life. It is plain and simple, it should never have happened to any of them, and I don't care if that is an argument in a bar, an unprovoked attack or a drug dealer whose been caught up in a sinful life. No one on this earth has the right to take someone else's life and play God in that way. Not in this country anyway, otherwise, the perpetrators would not be sitting in prison but would have paid for their crimes by having their own life taken.

It has come to a time in my life when I need to hand the baton over. I'm devastated that there is another runner in this race who can take up the fight because they too have lost their child just like me, but the reality is that I am tired. I forgot what it was like to actually live and feel happy. I felt guilty for laughing, smiling, having fun and loving, but I know that Andre would be proud of all that I have tried to contribute and for me writing this book has meant that I can tell his story. Not just all the parts that were visible to the public through articles, news, or my personal appearances, where I spoke about what I was going through, but all of it. The behind closed doors parts and the struggles that my family and I had to endure. It hasn't been easy, and there have been days when I just wanted the world to stop so I could get off. My entire life changed some parts for the better. I have met some fabulous people and changed my whole inner circle. I found the strength to deal with grief which I continue to use now in every aspect of my life. There are things that I will not tolerate in my life and will cut people and places off with the click of a finger. Some may think that is a selfish act, but I really don't mind being selfish if it means that I can have peace in my life and the ability to protect my loved ones. I have hurt beyond what I can describe, but I have also grown in confidence and understanding of the way that I want to live the rest of my life with my two children.

People have come into my life along the way, and I am forever grateful for the time and love they have shown. The fact that they left again is fine for me too. There is no animosity there. That's how life is. People come, and people go, unfortunately, but as long as the time they were in my life was good, it's okay for them to move on. I have a whole new circle of friends and have made massive changes from the things I thought would always remain in my life, but nothing is forever, and it now feels right to embrace new experiences and make changes when life becomes difficult. I guess that my new friends have picked up the baton from others and are now continuing the journey with me. It is a continuous journey because although I have found a new element of peace and acceptance, I am still heartbroken, and I don't think that feeling will ever change. There is no longer a gaping hole that hurts so badly that I feel as if I, too, am going to die from the pain, but there is definitely a scar that will never heal. It will be there forever, and I am sure of that.

From writing, I have brought myself clarity and laid some parts of what has happened in my life to rest. It has been like an ongoing therapy session. I have faced each part of the ordeal head-on and actually dug deep to write down my true feelings about all these parts. I have had to review and remember things that I had buried deep down so as not to cause a breakdown. It has taken me a long time to complete because, as I wrote, I would become emotionally drained and shut down; sometimes for months until I had the strength to evaluate why I chose to write this book in the first place and then find the power to continue again.

If you are reading this book and have also lost someone you loved, I hope it doesn't raise too many traumas for you. I hope you will see that you are not alone and that many of us have gone through this unfair experience. I also hope that you will know that time can start to heal, that life can continue, and that anything you choose to do, to keep your loved one's name alive is valid. It is also fine if you have chosen to close the door and live in private. We all deal with tragedies in our own way. If you are a parent with a child, you are worried about, please consider making the necessary changes to keep your child safe. I would have moved to Timbuktu if I had known that losing Andre was a real possibility. Losing possessions and lifestyles are no comparison to losing a child. Maybe read them some chapters of this book so that they realise what the reality looks like for a family and parent should things get so bad that a life is lost.

If you are reading this book because you have heard parts of my story and are just interested in listening to the facts, feelings and thoughts that have troubled my family and me for the last six years; that too is fine. I thank you for supporting my passion for sharing my son's story and keeping his name alive.

I pray for our young people every day and hope that someday, this madness known as knife crime will stop!

Yemi Hughes
Bereaved Mother of Andre Martell Aderemi.

CHAPTER 2
THE SHOOTING

I was exhausted. It had been a long day, and all that was on my mind was taking a long shower and jumping into bed. I climbed in and on the TV was my usual nightly watch, 24 hours in A&E. My two youngest boys were downstairs with their dad, and my eldest son was out as usual. I knew he was nearby; he never went far. I had spoken to him earlier in the evening to check whether he had walked our family pets. We had two Blue Staffordshire Bull Terroirs. A boy and a girl. We hadn't had them for very long, but they were already part of the family. They became protectors of the boys and had given the younger boys some responsibility with tasks such as walks and feeding. Life was normal, good. I finally had the family I always wanted, and I was grateful for that. even though there were ups and downs. I took the opportunity to get an earlier night than usual and must have fallen asleep to the sound of the boy's downstairs laughing and running around with their dad.

I woke abruptly by the phone next to the bed ringing loudly. I had missed the first call, but before I could call back, it was ringing again. I jumped up, not knowing what time of the night it was or how long I had been asleep. As the phone continued to flash, lighting up the room, I could see 'Andre Calling' on my phone's display. I instantly knew something must be wrong. Something had to be bothering him for Andre to call and not get hold of me and then call me back straight away. My son always called me first if there was a problem. Aside from that, he often called me throughout the day and night just to check in. I would laugh at him because it was as if he couldn't live without hearing me and knowing where I was. His friends referred to me as Andre's 'Ride or die', and sometimes they were shocked by the number of things I knew about their day-to-day lives, things that they maybe wouldn't tell their parents. Don't get me wrong, I was no pushover for any of them. If Andre were ever in the wrong, I would make it clear to him, but if he needed me, I would be there. Whether good or bad, we had a relationship where he understood that honesty was the best policy. This bond that we had was special.

I didn't have the same kind of bond with my other children, this was because, Andre and I together had experienced situations the others had not had to witness. It also wasn't that I loved Andre any more than the others, I loved them all equally, but we had reached a stage where Andre could be treated like an adult, so our relationship changed. He was my right-hand man, my confidante, and I loved him dearly.

Our mother-son relationship made my marriage harder. Andre was mostly always on my side and always looked out for me. It's not that I was always in an unhappy marriage, but Andre would tell me that I had changed and that I had become quite different. I was not my usual happy, bubbly self. I was very much an independent kind of woman. I didn't always get it right, and sometimes I found being a mother and a wife incredibly challenging. I always felt content and safe when Andre was around. His presence completed the house, and although sometimes this was quite dramatic, I always knew that his love for us, his family, was so important to him, and we always came first.

As I answered the phone, I could hear Andre's voice. It was low but sounded panicked. There was a tone to his voice that I had not heard from him that often.

"Mum, come now!" I sat up in bed and went into alert mode.

"What's happened? Where are you?" I replied, desperately trying to remain calm and get as much information from him as possible.

"At the Spar, mum, come now, please."

That was my son on the other end of the phone using a tone of voice that scared me. He was begging for me to come, and I knew that it was not good whatever situation he had found himself in. He didn't need to ask again. I hung up the phone and flew out of the bedroom in a panic. Dressed in my pyjamas, I headed down the stairs shouting on my way to anyone that could hear me.

"Where are my car keys? I need to go, something has happened to Andre". I screamed in what must have sounded like an urgent cry for help.

I grabbed my jacket, pulled on my shoes, and ran out of the house. I was terrified. I had no idea what was happening, but I knew by his voice that I needed to get there quickly. Behind me, I could hear my husband asking me to stop and calm down, but I knew I had to get to Andre as soon as possible. I didn't have the time to explain to him what Andre's call was about because I didn't really know myself. He was worried about me, and I understood his concern, but I didn't always think that he understood a mother's need to protect her children. He was always a little more cautious than me. He would evaluate the situation and then decide what should happen next in a rational way. I was the total opposite. If my boys needed me, I was there without thinking. However, this time felt a little different from any time before. I was scared about what I was about to encounter but knowing that Andre was talking and could call me reassured me that he was ok.

As I drove the short drive towards the Spar convenience shop, which was situated at the back of the estate, I noticed a car sitting in the middle of the road. It was a dark car, a black Mercedes. As I drove past the car, I noticed that the vehicle's occupants were young men. They were both slouched in their seats with the driver's window wound down. I continued to approach with caution before turning left into Freeland's Avenue. I wanted the boys in the car to see that I had noticed them. I found it strange that this type of car was being driven by such young-looking men. I couldn't work out why the car had just stopped on the road with the headlights on.

As a secondary school teacher, even though there were times that students could behave in quite an intimidating manner, I have always felt that I could handle them and any situations that I found myself in. I wasn't scared of young people. Not like how other people may feel intimidated when they see groups hanging around. I had a gut instinct that these boys were involved somehow in what was going on with Andre, but I was still none the wiser. Regardless of why they were there, it didn't feel very honourable. As I slowly approached the Spar, I was looking out for Andre. I didn't want to get out of the car,

fearing what might happen next. I kept checking my rear-view mirror to see if the vehicle I had seen was making any movements. The car was still stationary and still had its headlights on full beam.
I was desperately looking around. I needed to see my son, to make sure he was ok.

It was really dark. Only a few scattered streetlights and the trees lining the street were casting shadows across the ground. Out of the corner of my eye, I saw movement. As I focussed, I realised that it was Andre and he was with someone else, both were crouched down, and they were running towards my car. They were both trying to keep low to the ground and out of view. I instinctively leaned over the seat to pull open the passenger door, enabling them to get in quickly. My heart was racing. It was like a getaway scene from a movie. As they both approached, I realised he was with his friend Alex. Andre had a few friends with whom he had been friends for a while. Andre, Alex, Bradley, and Mark were the main group, and I had watched them grow up through their teenage years. I saw them start secondary school and then move on to college. I had known Bradley the longest. I taught him while carrying out my teacher training in a local school. I always described him as being the most troublesome one. Every time Andre was hanging out with Bradley, or if Bradley came to our house in the morning, just as I was leaving for work, there would always be a problem. He was a bit reckless. He had absolutely no filter and would just do or say some of the most stupid things at times. I often had to put Bradley in his place over our house, but he accepted it and always apologised. My husband had a gut instinct about him and always felt uncomfortable around him. He wasn't happy for Bradley to be over at our house, and maybe I should of, in hindsight, listened to him.

Alex was different. He wasn't the best-looking boy, but he had so much confidence in himself. This was often the joke in the house when they were bantering. He was quiet and very polite. For some reason, I was a little wary of him. He played his cards close to his chest, but I always pointed out to him that he was the one that I was keeping an eye on. Alex was heavily into Drill music. Alex's influence on music pulled the rest of the boys into that whole Drill scene. I had a great detest for Drill music. Even though I could see so much talent in some of the artists and their use of lyrics to create this style of music, I found that most of what I heard them regurgitating in the house was violent and portrayed a specific type of lifestyle which I feared. Mark, however, seemed to be quite sensible. I often came home and saw him in the front room playing FIFA with Andre. They used to take it so seriously, even to the point of placing bets. They would have their money on the coffee table, clearly gambling against each other all day.

"What is going on?" I screamed as I checked the rear-view mirror to see where the Mercedes was. I never expected to hear what Andre told me in a million years.

"Alex has been shot in the face, mum". He explained.

I spun around in my seat in total disbelief. Sat there in the dark in the back of the car was Alex with what looked like a wet face. Alex also lived on the estate. In fact, his house was closer than mine. It was apparent that he didn't want to go to his home with his face bleeding, and he also had no intention of making his mother aware of their situation. At the time, in the panicked mode I was in, I just wanted to leave the estate and get away from where we sat. Now that the boys were in their late teens, it was challenging to convince them to manage situations you thought were the best way. They were classed as adults and even though I had an honest relationship with Andre, I knew this wasn't the case with all of them and their parents.

"Oh my God! What is going on?" I screamed as tears started to fill my eyes.

I pulled off from where I had previously stopped, not knowing what direction I was heading. All I knew was that sitting there for too long may have found us all in additional danger. With my eyes flicking between the rear-view mirror and my son, who I was relieved was now sitting safely in the front, I noticed that the Mercedes had pulled off at the same time as me. My head was thumping as I tried to think of what was best to do, and my heart was beating fast in my chest. I needed to decide what to do quickly. Was this car going to continue following me? Was it involved in the shooting? Did they still have a gun? Where was I going? I was scared. So many questions whizzed through my mind. I could feel the tension in the car coming from both the boys. I was shaken but relieved that Alex was still talking, and that Andre appeared unharmed. As I drove off, I asked Andre to dial 999. I needed advice, as this wasn't the type of incident that I would be able to deal with alone. I didn't want to risk taking Alex to my house if the car followed me, and quite frankly, he needed to get to the hospital. As I turned the bend back onto Heathfield Vale, the Mercedes pulled out in front of me. I hit the break, and it sped off and turned right onto the main road heading towards Selsdon high street. By now, the Emergency Services were on the phone. They advised that they were sending Police. I went through what I believed had happened, and they advised me to go home. Both boys sat quietly in the car as if they were both in shock. This was a severe incident, and as boys that never really liked dealing with Police, tonight, they would not be able to avoid doing just that.

In recent years relationships had not been good between many young people on the estate and the local Police. I had been brought up with a different type of attitude to the one I noticed that young people of today have towards Police. I would always contact Police if I believed it to be necessary. Having a teenage son made me realise that there were difficulties and an apparent breakdown, and this often made it difficult to convince my son and his friends to report crimes committed against them. There had been violent incidents before where Police were called and either didn't respond, arrested them, or didn't show interest in what they were being told. Andre knew that I would contact Police, and he didn't try to stop me. Deep down inside, he knew it was the right way to respond. They knew the severity of what just happened and the danger not only to them but now to me, and the rest of my family and their prides were not going to stop me from doing the right thing at that moment.

I pulled up on my driveway and wrenched the handbrake up. Both boys climbed out of the car. I still felt nervous but safer now that I was home. My husband opened the front door, and I could see the expression on his face, disbelief at what he was seeing. Scared that we were being followed and worried that I was bringing Alex into my home with my younger children, I slammed the door before taking a deep breath. The look on the younger children's faces still bothers me today. I don't know what they must have thought, but I was even more horrified when we saw Alex for the first time in the bright lights of the livingroom. There were holes in his face, loads of small holes, from each hole red blood was bubbling, dripping down his face towards his chin. Some of the blood had started to dry onto his face. Alex had very dark skin, so even though the blood was visible, it didn't stand out like it would have on someone with fairer skin. His face looked swollen, and his mouth looked disfigured. His T-shirt was covered in blood, with drips of blood visible on his blue jeans and trainers. I felt sick. Andre's friends were always around me. I treated them as if they were my own children. They slept, ate, drank, and even came on holiday with us. I probably knew more about what was going on in their teenage lives than their own parents.

My family were now all gathered in the front room. My youngest, who was eight at the time, looked petrified. He didn't know what was happening and was concerned for the boy, who was also like a brother to him. Everything that was being said and everything that was being done, he had been exposed to it all. I could tell that he was taking everything in. My husband was displeased. I could tell by the look on his face. He wasn't Andre's biological father, and I felt that he would sometimes prefer me to just leave Andre and his friends to deal with whatever they may have been involved in and not be there for them. The need for a simple, peaceful life had ultimately always been the goal, but he was my son, my baby, even at nineteen, and there was no way I would ever turn my back on him and leave him in danger. The 999 operator was still on the phone giving updates. She advised me to collect a clean towel and hold it on Alex's face, which I was doing when the door started to bang loudly. As I pressed on Alex's face, I jumped, and my husband called out to the door.

"Who is it?" he inquired. With the answer coming back

"Police".

Now walking through my house were armed Police. They were carrying what I would describe as great big rifles. I knew very little about guns up until this point. The officers were huge and looked like real-life Action Men. No nonsense Police were coming in to assess the situation. After ordering us to remove our dogs from the front room, they made their way into where Alex was sitting.

Outside across the drive was a 4x4 Police Jeep and another two Police cars. Blue lights were flashing, and the neighbours were curtain-twitching. Police decided to request an ambulance which pulled up outside, and still holding the towel against his face Alex and I made our way out and climbed aboard. I had my first experience in the back of an ambulance. He was in pain but talking, which was a good sign, and in no time at all, we had arrived at St Georges Hospital in Tooting. Apart from childbirth and the odd occasion where I had to take one of the boys in for treatment after breaking a bone or injuring themselves in one way or another as they bounced around with no fear, I had never entered the A&E department before. I recognised my surroundings only from the TV show I watched religiously and had been watching that night. Being inside Resus was a strange experience. Exiting the ambulance and finally accompanying Alex inside, I reflected on the evening and worked out what had been happening.

It had been around 11pm, and Andre and Alex were sitting in their friend Bradley's car parked up on Freeland Avenue opposite the Spar food and wine shop. Andre was in the driver's seat, and Alex sat in the passenger seat next to him. They were in the car talking, waiting for Bradley to return, when another vehicle pulled up in front of them with the headlights on. Not knowing who was in the car, Alex decided to get out. As he stood shielded by the car door, trying to look beyond the bright lights, a figure appeared from the car in front and fired a shot which hit the window screen and sprayed out, hitting Alex in the face. Andre jumped out of the car, and together they ran to take shelter. It was at this point that he made the call for me to get him.

Speaking to the boys, I could tell that they were confused. They didn't know why someone had shot at them or who it could be. I could tell that they were trying to work things out, but at this point, they had not revealed any names or given anything about who they suspected was behind the attack. Police had already been to my house to speak to Andre about what he knew, and I was in regular contact with him on the phone. I stayed with Alex until I knew that he was comfortable and would be okay. After finding out the severity of his injuries, he contacted his family to tell them that he would remain in the hospital for the night and then it was time for me to leave. It was late, so I called a friend to pick me up, which she did and during the drive home, repeating the night's events seemed like I was talking about something that I had watched on the TV. Things like this don't happen in real life. People walking around with shotguns and shooting people in the face.

Saturday 16th July 2016, everything about the day had been normal up until now. What a night it had been. So far away from what I had initially intended. I was confused. I was nervous. I felt an unbearable anxiousness about the safety of all my children. As I reached home, I had a task to convince the boys that they were safe, and eventually, we all settled down to sleep.

CHAPTER 3
CRIMINAL DAMAGE

It was the day after the night before. Did all of this really happen? Nobody was leaving the house today, but this didn't stop the door from knocking continuously. There was a steady flow of Andre's friends arriving at the house. They had set up camp on the patio in the back garden. Luckily, it was a really nice sunny day. The garden umbrella was up and the windows in the downstairs of the house were all open. They were outside talking. I could hear them trying to work out what had happened the night before and I decided that it was best that I spent my time in the kitchen so that I could hear what they were saying through the windows without them knowing that I was secretly listening. Alex joined the boys later that afternoon. He had been discharged from hospital not requiring any surgery. He came to the house to collect his trainers which I had brought home with me from the hospital and more importantly to see his friends and let us all know that he was not too badly injured. The hospital had told him that it was lucky that one of the pellets hadn't entered his eye this could have left him blinded. The remaining pellets would work their own way out of his body through the surface of the skin so there was no need for them to be removed at the hospital.

His face looked terrible almost deformed. One side of his face was still swollen, this is where one of the pellets had entered his mouth chipping through his front teeth and had then become lodged in the inside of his mouth. With Alex discharged and back at our house the group of friends were reunited and the conversations about who was behind the attack continued. There were some clear confusions as to who was responsible for the shooting of Alex on the previous night but what was apparent was that they had not expected any type of retaliation from anyone. The only people that Andre and his friends had any type of conflict with were a group of boys that lived in Addiscombe and Shirley. This started in December 2015 and although there had been a number of confrontations between them there was nothing that the boys in my garden felt could have warranted a shooting to occur.

Our relationship was tight. Andre would always come home and tell me about his days. He knew I would be annoyed with him about some of the silly things he got up to but if he wanted my advice then he had to be honest. At no time during any of these conversations could I recall a time when I felt that Andre or anyone else's life had been in danger. It was all bravado. Boys buffing up their chests and trying to outsmart one another. They had all at one stage been friends, close friends or at least gone to the same schools so I could imagine them all saying very immature things to one another and playing what I can only describe as a game of one up.

"No way man, they ain't about that type of life", I heard Bradley say from the garden.

"How would they have got hold of a gun". It was baffling them.

"Fabio and Glare ain't going around shooting anyone, it must be that different yute that they are moving with now", said Alex.

"Yeah, well you said it was a silver Astra that pulled up in front of you, and that yute drives a silver Astra", said Carl.

"That's the one from Shrubland's, what's his name? Ali or something" Bradley replied.

"Yeah, him and Villain have been moving mad lately, but his ain't his beef so I don't know why he has started getting involved and cleaning up Fabio's shit", Alex added.

I was at the window trying not to let the boys know that I was listening to their conversation, but I was concerned about their safety, and I needed to know what was really going on. Every now and then I would go out into the garden and join in the conversation with them. They all trusted me. They spoke to me quite often about things that were troubling them. None of them liked to see me upset, angry or hurt. As I stood in the garden talks of more retaliation and even revenge became apparent. I just wanted this all to stop.

"You boys need to stop now and leave it; I don't want one of you to end up dead" I told them firmly.

From their faces I could see that they thought that I was slightly over exaggerating, but I meant every word. I had an instinct probably from the feeling that I got on the night when I arrived to pick the boys up. Those other young people sat in that car were watching, they must have been connected in some way and we had to live here.

"This is getting very serious and out of hand and I don't want anyone else coming to my house causing trouble", I said.

I needed to make them realise how serious things were especially when someone is willing to shoot at you. I went back inside and wrote down what I had heard so that I didn't forget anything and then carried on cooking. I enjoyed cooking for my family. We would all sit down together at the table and eat and having guests over or an extra person turning up as dinner was being served was something that I didn't mind at all.

As the day continued it became more apparent that there was information coming through on social media, that highlighted that indeed it was as the boys thought and that a boy named Ali and another going by the name of Villain were involved in the shooting of Alex. People were uploading Instagram's and snapchats laughing and sharing who was behind the incident of the night before. Before long there was a knock at the front door and as I opened it there stood two plain clothed officers with their ID badges open to show me. I let them in, and they explained that they needed to speak to Andre and Alex regarding the shooting. I knew the boys were not going to talk directly to Police. The culture of "Not snitching" was deeply imbedded in the youngsters that were at my house, so I had the feeling that I needed to intervene. I escorted the Officers into the living room so that I could speak to them in private before they went out to speak to the boys who were still working out who did what in the garden.

"Look, they are not going to speak up and give you any names", I explained.

"This culture of not stitching and dealing with things themselves which personally I think is ridiculous is not going to change, not today anyway"

I explained to the Officers, who were part of Trident, what I had heard the boys talking about in the garden for the best part of the day. I gave the name Fabio who I knew lived in Addiscombe and had previously attended Shirley High school. I gave them the name Ali, who apparently lived on Shrubland's Estate and drove a silver Astra which was the same car Andre and Alex had seen pull up in front of them. I also gave the names Glare and Villain, but I had no further details about either of them. I explained to the Officers that there had been ongoing issues with Andre and Fabio since their friendship had broken down in the summer of last year and asked them for help as I was scared about what might happen next. After speaking to me the Officers went out in the garden to speak to the boys.

"You alright lads, so what do you know about what happened last night?", they proceeded to ask.

Andre decided to speak first. He was always confident speaking to Police. They didn't bother him the way that I could see that Police presence was bothering the others.

"We were sitting in the car and a silver Astra pulled up in front of us and starting shooting what I think was a shot gun"

"Do you know who it was?" one of the Trident offices asked.

"No", Andre replied.

I expected none of the boys to talk because they never did. It infuriated me that they think that people's lives can be endangered by stupid, dangerous, life-threatening behaviour and not say anything because of their street code that the young people have created amongst themselves. What I didn't expect was the Officers response.

"Well lads let me tell you this. If there are any more shootings or any type of violent acts on this estate or in Croydon we will be coming back and arresting all of you".

I was fuming. Why would an officer that has already had me explain to them the mood, fear and thinking behind these young people then come in and make threats to arrest them when they have been subjected to crime and are ultimately the victims? I couldn't fathom how they felt that this was going to help to build trust or solve the crime. In fact, all this comment did was confirm the youngster's theory and strong belief that Police are not really interested and that they have only got each other's backs. We had a couple of normal days. Monday to Wednesday was quiet. Andre was not staying out late and was letting me know his whereabouts more than normal. End of term was approaching, and I had a spa day booked in for my first day off work. My husband was working nights and I was home with the boys. I was asleep in bed when I heard my door open and the light from the landing came shining in.

"Mum, Mum, Mum they are here", he whispered.

I heard a voice from the doorway. It was Andre. I sat up still half asleep to see him standing on the top of the landing holding the door open with one hand, and in the other hand by the side of his body was my husband's baseball bat. The light from the landing was beaming into the bedroom where my youngest was laying fast asleep next to me. I could only see a dark shadow leaning into the bedroom. Still blinded by the light, I jumped out of the bed and headed towards him. As I reached the landing, I could hear the sound of glass smashing.

"They are smashing up your car mum" he said, as we both headed down the stairs at a quick pace.

Andre still armed with the bat in his hand was heading for the front door. I had to stop him. I stood in front of the door blocking his way and instructed him not to go out there. There was a serious commotion going on, not only outside but inside too. Andre and I were arguing in the hallway about who was going to keep who safe if we went outside and on the other side of the door, you could hear total destruction happening. Glass was smashing and hitting the floor and what sounded like something battering the body work of the car. The noise coming from the attack that was going on outside had woken my younger children. They were now both standing in the front bedroom observing everything that was going on in the street outside, all made more visible by the lighting from the lamp post situated at the end of our driveway.

"You are not going out there!" I said, "and if you do, I'm coming too".

I knew that this would stop him. Andre hated the thought of me being in situations where I could be harmed. He would protect me to his death, and I would do the same for him. After several seconds I heard glass smashing in the living room. With the fear that someone could come into the house or even start shooting at us, I dialled 999 and asked for Police. Within minutes it was over and whoever they were, dressed in black and wearing ski masks with hoods up were now running across the road and jumping into a dark-coloured car and driving off with a screech. I waited a couple of minutes to make sure that they were really gone then we both cautiously made our way outside. I needed to see the damage to my car and the windows at the front of the house. I put the torch on, on my phone to enable me to get a better view and shone it around. The grass was glistening from the pieces of glass from the living room window and when I turned to look at my car, I couldn't believe what they had done.

The passenger side front window was completely shattered and had fallen inside. There was glass covering the seats and floor. The back window had also been completely smashed in. I could still hear pieces of glass breaking away from the frames and smashing on the ground and falling inside the car. There were dents everywhere. Each panel had been hit and I just couldn't believe that another incident had happened. CID Officers came to the house and spent some time outside taking photographs of the damage. They also managed to recover a broken hockey stick, half from inside the car and the other half from the grass in my front garden. As this was the second incident in the space of a week, CID asked me to stay at someone else's house for the night and they left.

I must have called my husband a thousand times that night and couldn't get hold of him. We had an argument earlier in the day and he had left for work. It was 4am, Police had left, and I was home alone with three children. Who was I going to call and wake up at this time of the morning? I did eventually call my mum to see if we could stay there for the rest of the night however, I couldn't drive my car because of the damage and the windows in the house were also broken. I made the decision to stay home. I tried to reassure the boys that they were safe and that no one was going to come back and in order for everyone to stay together, they laid on the sofa cuddled up to each other and fell asleep. I took the fleecy blankets always kept in the front room and covered them up. They were scared especially the younger ones. I pulled up the little red pouf and that is what I sat on for the rest of the night, watching over them like a lioness watching over her cubs. I was upset and angry. Whatever had been going on between these boys had always been kept on the street away from homes and families. What I had witnessed happening during the week had definitely escalated from anything that I first thought was low level bravado. All positions had changed. They were planning these attacks they were no longer spontaneous, and even going as far as coming to my home, scaring my children, and destroying my property. I gave the same information to CID Officers that night as I had previously given to Trident. There was no doubt in my mind that these two attacks came from the same group of people. I was becoming increasingly concerned for all of our safety. Was this going to be it now? Had they done their worst, or was there more to come?

The morning came quickly, and it was not long before the boys were awake, my husband was home, and the cleaning up began. For the first time in my life, I did not feel like my home was my castle. My home felt like an unsafe place where I was no longer in control over what could happen to us. I had to think fast about what the next steps were going to be because this was two incidents in a matter of days that Police were not taking seriously. There was a silence that was painful, my life had turned upside down and my children did not want to stay home, and I didn't blame them. Their safety was paramount, so I packed them up and sent them to my sisters.

CHAPTER 4
DRIVE BY SHOOTING

Thursday night, one empty house and a panic alarm. It had been decided that one should be fitted in our home because of the number of incidents that had occurred. Engineers came and fitted this big blue box to the corner of the house and talked me through how it worked. If there were any further threats, I could press the button on the control and police would be notified straight away. What was my life turning into? This was crazy. We are a normal family living on a normal street and now every other night there seems to be police in and out, people getting hurt and it was beginning to seem like all levels of normality had gone out of the window.

Andre had gone out to see his friends, I was a little annoyed because everything was up in the air. The children were sleeping away from home and the panic and paranoia I was feeling was real. As I sat watching the television my mobile began to buzz. Anytime I looked at the display on my phone and saw 'Andre' flash up my heart rate would go through the roof.

"Get away from the windows" he shouted.

As I backed away from the living room, where I had been lounged on the sofa with my back to the window, I turned and run upstairs. My heart was beating fast as I tried to comprehend what could possibly happen next. I did a mental check of everyone's whereabouts. I had seen blood and shootings and spent many nights awake recalling the scenes already. I did not know how much more I could truly take.

"They are shooting up the place by the Spar", Andre explained.

I went into the bedroom at the front of the house, where the boys had stood watching the madness unfold just nights earlier and peered out the window from behind the heavy curtains. I did not know if whoever he was referring to were heading to my house, so I stood watching keeping an air of caution. As I sat perched on the edge of the little one's bed, within minutes a moped slowly passed the house. Two passengers, one riding and one on the back. Grey tracksuit bottoms, white t-shirt, helmet, JD sports bag. Out the back of the JD bag I could see the butt of a shot gun. They did not stop. They looked at the house as they passed and carried on riding. Once I was sure that they were out of sight I grabbed my phone. Again, for another night, I had to call 999 and report a further incident to police. In my mind I could picture the riders speeding off the estate and heading down onto the dual carriageway. In my vision there were three police cars driving towards them with blue flashing lights trying to intercept them as they made their getaway. Finally, this would all be over, taken off the street, caught red-handed with the shot gun and locked away so no one could be hurt further. That never happened but how at times I wish it had, just the way that my mind had envisaged it.

The following morning, I received a call from police. I no longer felt that I could remain in my home, and after me having to convince them of that, they agreed for our safety we should move. I hated moving. I had been a parent for nineteen years and this was the third home that I had lived in during all that time. As my family grew and we needed more bedrooms, I had made the decision to move home for more space and a better standard of living. Originally from Old Town, Croydon, I had ventured to Upper Norwood where I spent several years on a quiet cul-de-sac with my two sons. After having my third child, I ventured to the opposite side of Croydon and found a three bedroomed house in Selsdon which I felt would be perfect for my family. For the first time I would have a drive to park my car on and the children would have a garden to play in. It was not until I had been living in the house for a few weeks that I ventured out one day to see what facilities were local. During that drive I realised that I had just moved onto a very large council estate. The further from the main road that I travelled, the more houses and flats that I found. There was a local convenience store, a secondary school, youth club and a park. I had lived in Croydon all my life and never even knew that this estate existed. It felt like an adventure, a fresh start, a nearly forever home.

Being a teacher in a local school, there were many young people that lived on the same estate. They called me 'Miss' at school and 'Aunty' when they were spending time together with my own children in the garden or whizzing up and down on their bikes. I got to know their families and they became part of mine. I cannot say that my boys did not have a good childhood growing up on Monks Hill. Everyone knew us, we were part of the community and we always felt safe and happy. What was happening now, was happening from people outside of our community They did not live here. They did not belong here. These people were causing chaos and I was now seriously considering moving away and starting over. I had no idea how to make this happen. I did not have the money or the ability to move at the click of a finger. I knew that trying to move would be a big chore, but I also knew that this needed to happen for our own safety. Police emailed me a letter and told me to take it to Croydon Council the following morning and see if they were able to assist with finding alternative suitable accommodation.

I sat in that office all day. A mixture of different types of people were contained inside little meeting pods putting their cases forwarded for being housed. I really hate and resent the systems of affordable housing. These people at the council can change your future. To place you somewhere that they think is suitable for you, to turn you away if they think you don't meet their criteria or believe that you can help yourself in some way or another. I looked at their faces I never really thought that I was different from any of them but now I actually saw myself thinking hard about what each of these people's different circumstances were. I was living in a world that I didn't recognise anymore when life used to be so simple and being happy and feeling free was a thing of the past. I also realised that there were a lot of people that were running from wars and different situations where they too felt unsafe and the error of judgement that we often have as we look at these people and believe that they don't have the same rights to safety and freedom as we do. Now that my safety and freedom was in jeopardy, I needed that help too I haven't lived in a council property for a number of years, and this was a very scary venture, but I had no other options. I had to ask for help and try to get the support that I needed. My family's future was in the hands of these people that I didn't even know.

I sat there all day, waiting patiently for my turn to put my case forward. Myself, my husband, Andre, Ashley, and Amari really needed that place to go too in order to feel safe. I couldn't bear to have another night without the boys all being under the same roof. I needed to be able to sleep at night knowing that nobody was going to run up in our home or even worse shoot or a stab one of my children and cause them harm. It was getting late; the office was becoming deserted, and they were about to close. Only the security guard was left hanging around to ensure no one else entered the building as the working day came to an end. Finally, I was called to one of those pods to meet with the advisor to whom I had earlier put my case. They had made the decision to offer my family emergency accommodation and I was handed an envelope which listed the occupants for the landlord. The advisor explained to me that the only place that they had suitable would involve an immediate move to Kent. I sat staring at here map that I was given. Gillingham, Kent that just seemed like so far away. It felt like I was being sent to the other side of the world and to be honest I didn't really know what to expect. I had never considered the possibility of having to move out of London during my entire time sat in those offices. I'd never lived outside of London before. In fact, I'd never even lived outside of Croydon, how was I going to cope being so far away from everything that I knew.

A million and one thoughts rushed through my brain. The most crucial question I was asking myself was how I was supposed to get to work. I knew that I had no choice if I wanted to keep my family together and safe. I needed to take this opportunity that they were giving to me and try to work out all the more intimate details later. The advisor that worked at the council addressed me in a very matter of fact way about the decision.

'You need to go to the property to collect the key and you need to go today', she told me. 'You can't take anything with you, none of your own furniture, you can only take what you need, clothing and bedding, but you will see what you might need when you visit the property"

It was scary to think that I was going to have to go to an area that I had never been to before and try to restart my life. I agreed to what I had been told and signed the paperwork for the property. I came out of the council office with a feeling that was bittersweet. The sweet bit was being given the opportunity to go away and start afresh without all the fears that I had experienced the last few weeks. It was the understanding that nobody would know where we lived, and nobody would just be able to turn up there at whatever hour of the day or night when they felt and attack my family. The bitter bit was that I had made a family home already. I had a nice home, a family and somewhere where we were happy once. This was a place where before all of this madness started, I was comfortable to sleep in my bed at night. I could leave the back door unlocked and I still felt safe. I felt like I knew everybody, and all of this security was going to disappear and there would be no turning back. If I left this house that I had been renting for the past eight years and moved to Kent, then there was no coming back. The house would be gone. The house would no longer be somewhere where we could live again when and if this situation calmed down. My friend agreed to drive me to the property to meet the agent so that we could collect the keys and work out what I needed to take to the new house.

We pulled up on this peaceful little cul-de-sac. There were these quaint little houses each with their own garages located in a separate area at the rear of each house. My initial thoughts were that this seemed like a quiet little neighbourhood that housed families that cared about where they lived. Most of all, it felt safe. There were nice cars on driveways, nicely kempt homes with tidy front gardens and most of all it was peaceful. There was no noise coming from the road nor the houses. I met with the agent who handed me the keys and I made my way inside. I opened the front door to a small entrance hall which was brightly lit up from all the windows and natural light. Directly in front of me was the carpeted staircase leading to the bedrooms upstairs. The patterned reddish carpet stood out against the white walls and was bright, clean and it was very cosy. Slightly to the right was a doorway which led directly into the living room all that was in there was a dirty red coloured leather sofa with two armchairs and a rather large white mantlepiece with a marble base which expanded out across the wooden flooring.

We continued moving on through the living room which led into the kitchen. The kitchen was nicely laid out and very bright with big windows above the sink. I actually hated the kitchen at Heathfield, the layout of it was ridiculous for its size, there was hardly any worktop surface and the oven had been perched inside its housing and had never been securely fitted in place. In fact, I had to do some feminine DIY which actually did do the job eventually. I ended up perching the oven in the space on top of an upside-down saucepan and screwed the front in place using some normal house screws. In comparison to the Heathfield house this kitchen definitely was the type of kitchen that I wanted to be a mother and a wife in and cook those family meals that I enjoyed doing so much. I could see myself in there, keeping busy. Everything was integrated, the washing machine, dish washer and there were even drawers to put the cutlery in, that was something that the Heathfield house never had. Having no drawers meant that everything needed to be kept in boxes inside cupboards; all the cutlery, knives, and every piece of kitchen equipment that you would normally keep in a kitchen drawer had to be stored in the most unusual places.

In the kitchen were patio doors which opened up into a small neatly designed garden which had a nice decking area and then grass that framed the pathway that led you down to the back gate. This gate, when opened took you out to the garages where every house had allocated parking. Even though I was forty-five miles away from home I felt like I could make this place home so I decided then and there that this would be the place that we would move to in order to keep my family safe and have a fresh start. I had a million different thoughts going through my head it was the start of the summer holidays after all and being a teacher meant that I had about six weeks to play with, to try and organise my family and how we would get to and from school on our return in September. It was a scary time I've never lived so far away from my mum and my sisters before but as a mother I knew that I needed to do what I could to keep my children safe.

It was after about two days that I was finally able to arrange the move. We had spent days packing boxes, sorting through rubbish, and deciding what we needed to take to the new home, what needed to stay in storage and what needed to be thrown away. The family rallied around to help and as we sorted through old photographs, we found ourselves reminiscing about the past, some of the happier days. Packing things into boxes and the reality that we were leaving our family home became real. It was a very tearful time for us all, but I knew this was the step that I needed to take to try to keep us all safe and together. There was no turning back once this decision had been made, the minute that I handed back the keys to this home it would close that door forever. I organised storage and hired a van. Once the date to move had been finalised it was all go.

The day of the big move arrived. The hardest part of that day was the morning when my friend came to collect our dogs. She had arranged for them to be rehoused because the property that we were going into did not allow for any pets to live there. The four of us stood in silence in the middle of the street as she loaded their bedding and their cage into the boot of her car. We were losing a part of our family. They were both so friendly, we loved them, and this was such a hard thing to do. As I watched the boys looking at the dogs jumping into the back seat of her car getting ready to leave, I got an emotional lump in my throat. I think the intention at this time was that once we had become settled and got a more permanent home that we'd be able to get them back. The female dog Diesel who was slightly older than the male dog was definitely in control. On many days she would lay there in the garden, stretched out in the sun watching as the boys ran up and down with the boisterous younger dog called Zeus. I was forever shouting at them.

"Will you stop hyping those dogs up, I need them to be calm not wanting to chase everything insight and jump all over the place", I would demand.

Andre's idea of walking the dogs was taking them out for a late-night walk and training them to chase the Fox's. We had an array of wildlife where we lived and, on any night, you could see anything from foxes to badgers. The other two boys thought this was hilarious. Of course, it wasn't and the stories I used to hear from them when they came back about the chases that Zeus would give when he was let off his lead. The boys felt protected when they were out with the dogs. They gave our home a sense of security.

One day my husband called me at work to tell me that he'd lost the dog, straight away I knew it was Zeus. He'd been in the garden taking in the washing and they had both been out there running around and enjoying the freedom until Diesel the female dog decided to just sit down and relax in the sun leaving Zeus to entertain himself. My husband had gone inside to put the washing down and when he'd come back out it was only Diesel left. Zeus had disappeared through a hole in a fence in the fence and made a run for it. I was in a panic after receiving the call and quickly made my way home to start the search for the dog. Because both dogs were similar, I thought it was best to take Diesel out on her lead, hoping that someone was going to recognise that we had a Blue Staff and would spark a conversation about Zeus being missing. The first time we lost Zeus I was directed by a lady who had found him wandering the streets alone so stopped to collect him. He was quite happy to jump in the back of her car and drive off without a care in the world. Diesel was never this inquisitive she wouldn't go anywhere unless you had said she could. After about an hour and a half of searching for Zeus, I gave up and came back home. I just didn't know what else to do. I had a similar feeling the day that I lost Ashley in Dulwich Park when he was about four years old. The only difference was I knew that Ashley could speak and could say who his mum was, there was no way anyone was going to know that Zeus belonged to us, and I feared that we had permanently lost him.

I went home to break the news to Andre that I couldn't find him and that I needed to get back to work. I had no idea where the dog could have gone.

"Mum, on your way back to work, stop off at the vets and let them know that he's gone missing because somebody might bring him in", Andre asked me.

I thought it was highly unlikely, but I did just that. I walked into the vet which was situated on our local high street and asked the lady at the front desk if a missing dog had been brought in.

"What is the name of your dog?" She asked

"Zeus, he's a Blue Staff", I replied.

The lady started to smile and then notified me that he was there. He was out the back of the veterinary practice being spoilt rotten by some other members of staff. The relief that I felt knowing that he was safe was crazy considering I didn't really want them in the first place. I never thought that I would ever grow a bond with these dogs. I'm not a dog lover I never grew up with dogs as a child. We had a cat and the odd occasion my mum would buy us a budgie or some fish, but we weren't pet people. For some reason these two had grown on me and I don't know why, but even though they were hard to maintain I loved the joy that they brought to all three of my children. Out comes this crazy dog. He runs from the back of the vet to where I am standing waiting for him. He looked at me as I called his name.

"Zeus you're such a naughty boy, where have you been? Why did you run off like that?", I asked as I kneeled to greet him.

He jumped up on me happy to see me and then in a blink of an eye he had ran back from where he had just come from. I stood there with a strange look on my face. He was being fed all sorts of treats out the back and he was quite enjoying himself. I finally got him into the car and took him home to Andre who was over the moon to see him. Diesel on the other hand was not impressed that we had bought him back and she just turned her nose up and snuggled down to get comfortable on the bed that they shared.

We got on with the day. We started by filling the van up with all our belongings that we were going to dispose of at the dump. Andre had totally decimated his bedroom I don't think there was anything left that he had intended to carry. He smashed his bed to pieces and took great pride in ensuring that every piece of it was unrecognisable. He threw his clothes into a few black sacks and put them into the room full of the things that we needed to keep. As we filled the van up with the rubbish ready to take to the dump the reality of us moving was creeping up on me. We had so much to get rid of and this really was the reflection of the many years that we had lived here. Once we were finished and all the rubbish had been removed it was time to pack the things that we needed to keep and take those to the storage unit. It was hard work lifting, moving, packing, and stacking all day long but it was necessary, and we just needed to get it done.

We finally arrived at the new house and was able to begin to unpack the little things that we had chosen to bring with us. The house was bare, it didn't feel like a family home we had nothing that was personal just the necessities that we needed to get through the summer. Here we were in a new house in a strange area, and nothing felt familiar anymore. No family portraits on the walls, no rugs and none of our bits and bobs that made us feel comfortable. We spent the first few days exploring the neighbourhood. There were many little shopping and entertainment centres locally with different activities for the children to take part in such as ice skating and boating. There was a lovely shopping centre within a short drive from where we were living, some great parks and a couple of leisure centres which housed swimming pools with water slides and lazy rivers. After a couple of days of exploring the new neighbourhood and getting settled in, the dread of being so far away from home started to creep in.

CHAPTER FIVE
A LONG WAY FROM HOME

The first few days felt like a holiday, in fact it was the first week of the school summer holidays and I felt relaxed. When you move away to a new area people start to make plans to visit and spend time with you. Had this been a normal move, under different circumstances I would have welcomed visitors. In true Heathfield style I would have cracked open the BBQ and welcomed my friends and family to the neighbourhood. This would have been lovely because the house and garden were both quite impressive in comparison to where we had come from, but there were so many conditions when taking the property from the council it was beginning to feel near impossible to actually settle down and make the most of this new adventure. Don't get me wrong, there was nothing physically wrong with the home we had. It was homely and we were able to build some great memories there as a family. Some private landlords leave a lot to be desired and whilst I appreciated the fact that my landlord just left us alone to get on with our lives, I didn't appreciate his lack of motivation to complete the work that was very much needed. Nevertheless, Heathfield was home. It was big enough for us to host Christmas day dinners and birthday parties. New Year's Eve celebrations were always held at mine for all the family, and we had great neighbours who never complained about my husband's bass speakers or the number of children from the estate who constantly popped in or out.

One evening we were sat on the sofa trying to watch normal TV. There was no Internet at the new house and the signal for accessing your normal one to five or Freeview channels was proving to be a challenge at the best of times. Andre had coerced us into buying a wireless internet device and a Now TV box but on the first night of watching a family movie the data ran out within thirty minutes. As we sat, there was a bang at the front door, the type that you would expect from Police. We were sat in silence looking at each other wondering who it could possibly be. We didn't know anyone in the local area, and we definitely were not expecting visitors. My husband got up off the sofa to answer the door and stood there, on the doorstep, was the man from the letting agency. We welcomed him in, not that we had much choice and waited patiently to hear from him what had sparked the sudden late at night.

"Good evening", he said. "We have had a complaint from the neighbours about noise coming from this property"

I sat there looking at him in disbelief. Apart from the odd play fight that the boys had, there really was no noise coming from this house.

"Your neighbour works night shifts, and he can hear you throughout the day going up and down the stairs", he continued.

I know that if I were in the same situation now, as I was then, I would have responded in a totally different way. Because our neighbour was a night worker, he thought it was okay to make a complaint with the landlord that we were making too much noise in the house during the day. It would have been impossible for us to stay downstairs for the entire day and tiptoe around. It didn't help I suppose that the house was hollow, empty, not filled with any furniture. It wasn't as if we were deliberately indulging in noisy activities or inviting the community around for a house party (the type of thing we could have happily done at Heathfield). The complaint was that we were making too much noise going up and down the stairs. This actually made me chuckle because at Heathfield we were the life and soul of the street. People continuously coming in and out music playing, children screaming in the garden as they laughed and played, dogs barking. We had never had such a complaint before and to be honest it was ridiculous.

"I'm sorry to tell you, but if I get any more complaints about any noise, and that includes going up and down the stairs in the day, I will have no choice but to contact the council and let him know that you can't live here", he enforced.

This was shocking considering we weren't making any noise and there was nothing to make noise with inside the house, not even a radio.

"You know the people round here they've watched programmes like benefits Britain and if they catch on that you've been moved here by Croydon Council, they're not going to be very happy", he said.

I was in total disbelief as to what was coming out of this man's mouth. I sat gob smacked, mouth wide open, looking at my husband. I couldn't actually believe what I was hearing. The level of disrespect that we as a family was having to take because we were put into a vulnerable situation. This was the biggest amount of discrimination and judgement I've ever received in my lifetime. The fact that we were paying thirteen hundred pounds a month to live in an empty house that I wasn't even allowed to bring my own furniture to, had no Internet access or services and couldn't even have a friend or family member stay over and now I was being told that we couldn't even move up and down the stairs during the daytime was an absolute joke.

"Excuse me, what do you mean benefits Britain? I'm not living on benefits and even if I was that is nobody's business. I'm actually a teacher so I'm entitled to be at home right now it is the summer holidays after all", I responded trying to remain calm.

"Look love, I don't care what you do for a living just make sure you don't tell the neighbours anything about your circumstances. If any of them ask you tell him that you're a nurse and that you'll be starting at Medway hospital soon", he stated.

I was absolutely fuming. Besides from this feeling of anger and disbelief of total arrogance that this landlord was showing, I was actually scared for our future. I had given up my family home that I'd lived in for ten years and moved all the way to this unfamiliar area in the hope to change the situation that we were in and now I had this man talking to me about benefit Britain and being a nurse at Medway. He continued to tell me that we would have to move back to Croydon and live in bed and breakfast which absolutely petrified me. Not only because Croydon didn't feel safe for us right now, but also, because I needed to keep my family together. I knew that if we were placed in temporary accommodation such as bed and breakfast, we would all be split up. My husband most probably would have to live in accommodation with the eldest two boys and myself and the youngest one who was only eight would be put somewhere else. This would totally split my family up and right now, we needed each other. This was a fear that I was allowing this man who knew nothing about our family's situation to put me in. There was nothing I could do about it so from this moment on I lived each day on eggshells. Things had already been rocky between me and my husband and this extra pressure of us living in this type of environment just added to the strain that was already there. This move was a chance for us to try to work things out away from all the distractions, but it wasn't long before we began arguing again. The arguing and the noise that this was creating made me fearful. I used to plead with him to stop shouting, because I had a genuine anxiety that at any moment this landlord could pull the rug from underneath our feet and send us into a whirlpool of even more uncertainty.

It was about midday, and I was stood in the kitchen when I heard a noise behind me. I turned around suddenly and there was my husband stood with two bags and a suitcase. He had been upstairs and made the decision to pack his belongings and leave us. Within minutes the back gate opened and there stood an old friend of his who had come all the way to pick him up and drop him back to Croydon.

"I'm not staying here any longer, you're on your own" he said.

His friend helped him with his bags, and they disappeared out the back gate and that was it he left us in Kent and went back to Croydon. I didn't have the energy to question him on his actions. We had all been through so much, lost so much and the pressure of day to day living underneath each other was driving us all crazy. Everything seemed like bad timing. My husband's car had broken down a few weeks before we had to move so this restricted his ability to move around freely as he wished. He had also been in a temporary night job in Croydon before we moved so he had to give that up too. I can only imagine the frustration that he must have felt as a man, husband and father knowing that all of these events were happening and there was nothing that he could do to stop it. I didn't ask him to stay or argue with him, I just let him go. I had been left on my own so many times in my life to fend for myself and my children, it wasn't a situation with which I was unfamiliar. If I have done it before, I could do it again and I truly believed that as things worked themselves out, we could, as a couple, try to resolve our marriage issues and get our normal family life back.

Now the loneliness really did start to set in. Apart from the one day that my sister had driven to Kent to visit, we hadn't seen anyone. Because of the situation at the house, we had chosen to take the children swimming. We couldn't even invite them back to the house afterwards to play or to eat because I was scared about what the neighbours would think and complain about. I wasn't sure of the lengths that they would go to in order to report us to the housing people, but I wasn't willing to take any risks. After the trip to swimming, the men took the boys for a kick around in the park before they got themselves ready to head off home and leave us once again in this strange place. On reflection, I really do think that if I had been able to have visitors stay over like my nephews it would have made the transition easier for the boys. They would have been able to have come and stayed and played with the boys and this would have given them something to do, and it would have helped with the settling in process. We had thought about sneaking my children's friends in especially once my husband had left but we knew that we couldn't take the risk.

The cost of moving had bankrupted me for the month. I was desperately waiting for payday to come then maybe I would be able to do more things with the children. We could make more use of the local facilities so that they could enjoy their summer. The month was moving really slowly, and we were all becoming very bored. The desire to go back to Croydon was growing and whilst we were out in the town centre one afternoon Andre realised that there was a train station called Gillingham. After further investigation he realised that if he jumped on the train at Gillingham he could be in Bromley within minutes. This was the start of Andre leaving us at home and travelling back to Croydon to meet up with some of his friends. This angered me, I was furious. I had packed up my home and moved forty-five miles away not only for my husband to get up and leave but also for the son that I was trying to protect so badly to then decide that he was just going to disappear off too. I was desperate for just some normality to my life, a weekend out with my friends a normal day in a normal house it just all seemed too much to ask for.

One of the days when we had been left home alone, me and the younger two children took a trip down to the local shopping centre to break up the day. As we looked around, we noticed that there was an EE phone store and it had totally slipped my mind that I was due an upgrade. I went into the shop and the boys helped to look at suitable phones, I walked out with a brand-new contract. I know it sounds really silly but having no money and being in a situation where you're so far away from where you really want to be, these little things give you a temporary happiness. Something to look forward to and something new to focus on for a short period of time. I spent that night playing around with my phone, it hadn't been SIM activated yet, but I was advised that this would happen in the next 24hrs once the SIM card was inserted. I swapped over my WhatsApp and waited patiently for my new phone to switchover. The next morning the phone still hadn't switched over, so we took the short drive back to the EE store to enquire whether there was an issue or not. They notified me that there was a problem with their systems and therefore I would have to wait a little bit longer before my new SIM was activated. I really wouldn't have minded but to make the situation even more unbearable they disconnected my phone number completely. I was livid. How could they allow this to happen? I know that they were not privy to my personal circumstances, but I wanted to blame them for taking away the only connection that I had to the outside world. For the first time in my life, I felt like a prisoner. Locked up with no contact, no Internet, no Wi-Fi, and no phone. No husband around, no grown-up son at home, just me and the two little ones. The next day I called them again and they suggested I return to the store to get a temporary SIM for the phone so that at least people would be able to contact me, if need be, I still had access to the WhatsApp, so I was able to take and receive calls through that but without having Internet in your home it becomes a costly extra expense topping up data.

The next few days were challenging. My friend and her son drove down to visit us, and we took the children to the beach, if that's what you can call it. It was supposed to be a blue flag beach, but the beach only had dirty sea water and pebbles. It was lovely to get out and about and at this time I really appreciated the efforts that my true friends were making to keep me grounded during this crazy time. It was lovely to watch the children playing in the sand filled play area, laughing, and smiling as though all they had witnessed back in Croydon hadn't happened. Amari was so young and in a short space of time he had been subjected to so many different incidents and I could see that some of the day-to-day aspects of life such as bedtime routines were affecting him. How could he feel safe and happy when he had witnessed people turning up in the middle of the night to smash the house to pieces? How could such a young person recover from seeing blood pouring out of the face of someone he knew? I was worried that without the support and connections to those that we loved he wouldn't recover from the traumas that he had seen, but I was going to do my best to try and make him feel safe in his home no matter what.

CHAPTER SIX
16TH AUGUST PART 1

I woke up early. It was a funny kind of day; I had no real plans, and all three boys were in an irritable but playful mood. After taking a shower, I was desperately trying to relax on the bed wrapped in a bright red towel, but my youngest Amari decided to join me still in his playful mood. He kept coming into the bedroom to deliberately irritate me. He was collecting an assortment of things from around the house and bringing them for me to look at. He had a shiny pendent which he was swinging so close to my face for me to look at I was sure it was going to take my eye out. On top of this he had the camera on, on the useless mobile phone that I had and was singing and recording the annoying acts as he went. I cherish these memories now. I hadn't felt this low for quite a while. The lack of routine was beginning to kick in not just for me but for everybody. To escape briefly I sat in the garden and contemplated what I could do with myself for the day. Andre had been away for the last couple of days visiting friends. Not in Croydon but other friends that he hadn't seen for quite a while. These were the type of friends that he had gone to school with. Even though they may not see each other often they refer to each other as being brothers. I think that with all the turmoil that was going on in our lives, he missed them. It's funny how you can have long lasting bonds with people and although you are not regularly in contact when you meet back up it's as if you have never been apart. I was still furious with him for leaving us in Kent alone and had spent the morning reminding him that we were there as a family to keep him safe.

I didn't have much credit on the 'temporary' phone that EE had given me, but I needed to hear the voices of those I would often turn to for guidance and support. I made a few phone calls, the call me back type, because I don't have any credit. The first call I made was to my sister-in-law. We were very close. We had lived next door to each other for several years on a quiet leafy cul-de-sac in Upper Norwood. Those were the good old days. A community of mothers bringing up their children, leaning on and supporting each other. Her youngest daughter and Andre were the same age and they had grown up together. Their relationship was special. They had shared many milestones together and as they got older the memories between them were immense. There were nights I would come home and see Melissa sat outside my house at Heathfield talking to Andre who was in the passenger seat. I loved their closeness it was more like brother and sister than cousins. Andre scrutinised any male who got close to Mel and Mel did the same back. She would lecture Andre on a range of different aspects of his life which she found irritating, but they always ended their conversations with a hug.

My sister-in-law over the years had been more like an adoptive mum. Someone who would listen and give me advice about all those things that I couldn't talk to my own mum about. Even though her and my mum were roughly the same age, give or take a few years she had a younger outlook on life. She was still dressing up and partying and taking adventurous holidays abroad. Her makeup and dress sense were on point, and she was definitely an independent kind of women. My mum had settled down and got re-married and was living a more peaceful life. My sister-in-law and I would go on holiday together, attend events and be up until all hours of the morning reasoning about the wrongs in my life. I didn't see her as my sister-in-law I always just referred to her as being my big sister and in times of need, especially when I was feeling down, she would always be someone that I could lean on.

Going back to visit The Lawns was always like returning home. It was a place of safety, it was somewhere that I was familiar with and even though I had to walk past my old front door to visit her, I still got a sense of comfort from being there. I should have stayed living there. I never should have moved to the house at Heathfield. It would have been a squash having three children in a two-bedroom flat, but I could have made it work somehow. At least I would have had that support from someone who would have been able to have guided me and helped me with the children as they hit those teenage years. We had a brief conversation. Mandy was the manager of a wine bar in Streatham, and she was working that night. It was a Tuesday night, a night known as Caribbean renaissance. We talked about me coming down for a night out and leaving the children at home. When I lived at Heathfield having a much-needed night out was never an issue.

Even if my husband didn't want to watch the children for the evening, I had my 19-year-old son that was grown up and always willing and able to stay home with the other two. Andre didn't go out much, in fact he very rarely left the estate that we lived on. If I called him, he would be back at the house within 5 minutes.

After being a single mum for so many years this was something that I valued. There had been nights where I'd wanted to go out but had no one to watch the boys especially when the two oldest ones were young. This was no longer an issue now the eldest had come of age, he was mature enough to stay home and look after his brothers. My girlfriends and I had a rule that if we went on a night out, we always had to get up early enough the next morning to make sure that the dinner was cooked, and the house was clean ready to start a new week. Sometimes we would be exhausted but if the weather were good, we would take the children to the park in the late afternoon to let them run around and play together whilst we relaxed and recovered from the night before. There are some good memories of our trips to the park to entertain the children after dinner. We enjoyed our weekends, but the children enjoyed them more.

I was contemplating jumping in my car and driving down to Croydon later that evening for a few hours and then returning the same night or early in the morning before the children woke up. I needed escapism, just to dip my toes back into the world, which was my reality, which at the time felt so far away from the way that I was now living. For the first time in a long time, I felt so isolated, so alone, it was like I was in a nightmare. This wasn't really what I had planned. I wasn't used to being so far away from everybody that I loved or not being able to just pop down the road to visit somebody when I felt like it. I know it was getting to Andre too and it had already got to my husband hence the reason he left and headed back to what he knew. The younger two were just going along with it all, but today felt different not just for me but them too.

As the day drew on the boys become even more restless. The little one was fighting with the big one, the big one was fighting with the middle one. They were running around making so much noise. I was concerned that I would get that dreaded knock on the door to complain about the noise and be faced with the threat that we needed to leave. After another phone call I decided that I wouldn't just go down to Croydon on my own that evening and that I would take them all with me. We all needed a break from one another and needed to interact with some other people. I would drive down to my sister-in-law's house and go to work with her that evening. The boys would stay at her house and then the following evening we would go to my mums and spend a couple of nights there before returning to Kent. The boys agreed that they would come. Ashley and Amari we're excited, it was like a little adventure and finally they were going to get see some people that they hadn't seen for a few weeks. Maybe they would even get to see their dad, because they hadn't really spoken to him since he left us there that day. There was no rush, finally having a plan put a degree of calm on us all. Knowing that we were going to visit family elevated the level of anxiety and frustration that we were all feeling. We were casually getting ready. They were running baths and throwing a few things into bags. I was upstairs organising myself and pottering around and Andre called up the stairs.

"Mum, what shall we do about this food that's in the fridge? If we're going to be away for a few days, should I cook it and do some food before we go", he said.

Andre loved being in the kitchen he had this little knack of being able to create something out of nothing. I would look in the cupboards and fridge and say that there was nothing to eat, but he would look and see lots of ingredients that he could conjure together to make a meal fit for a king. I always thought that he would go on to study to be a chef, he just had this natural talent of combining ingredients. If we had no bread, he would pull out flour and make flat bread. He could rustle up something in the middle of the night if he was hungry or he could scrape loads of things together and make us all dinner. After about 30 minutes he called us downstairs to the kitchen where he had been cooking up a storm in the kitchen. As we were going away, he just decided that anything that was left he would cook it and we all sat down together to eat. It was really nice, sat around the table together talking, eating, and just laughing with each other.

This is something that we hadn't done for a very long time, and I'd missed it. As the evening drew closer, we decided that we would leave out about half past six, so everybody started to get their things together. Andre had loaded all the plates and cutlery into the dishwasher, and I was putting the bins out and doing the last bit of cleaning up when Andre came downstairs with a pair of jeans and a tee shirt in his hand.

"Mum, do you think you could iron these for me?", he asked.

This was a bit of a strange request. Andre, ironing clothes. He wasn't that fussed about ironing his clothes and I suppose where we were used to having the washing machine and the tumble dryer, he would just throw them in, and it come out wrinkle free.

"You know where the iron is Son" I joked.

This was a boy that I just could not resist doing everything for. He just had to smile at me with that big smile and perfectly straight white teeth and my heart would melt. This annoyed my husband to be fair, Andre definitely had the charm to win anybody over and that included me, his mum. He gave me his clothes, a pair of dark blue jeans and a bright blue north face tee shirt. It was hot outside, even though it was getting later in the afternoon the sun had stayed really hot. Once we were all ready to leave, we headed out the back door to get into the car and that's when bedlam broke out. Amari had my car keys, and he was running round and round the car on the gravel pavement. He wouldn't unlock the car and wouldn't give the keys to Andre who was demanding them. Amari was laughing so hard as he tried to avoid being caught by his brother. Ashley was like the piggy in the middle. He didn't know what to do. Should he get involved and try to help get the key or stand there with his hands up remaining on natural ground. Then just like that there was a bang and Amari hit the ground. Now Amari was bleeding and screaming, Andre was repeating 'I told him to stop!' and Ashley was already strapped in the back seat of the car still not getting involved.

Upon closer inspection I noticed that Amari's arm was bleeding around the elbow area. There was some grit and scrapped skin on his knee. I promised I would stop at the petrol station to get him some special wipes and a plaster and with that he jumped into the back of the car and strapped in.

The drive to Croydon normally took approximately 45 minutes. As we headed out, in went a CD full of UpToDate tracks from a range of genres and our journey began. As I drove, windows down we sang aloud in the car. After about 20 minutes as we hit the motorway, Andre was asleep in the passenger seat, Amari had finally settled and began to doze off too and Ashley and I was left to take in the view as we continued on our journey. Andre was wearing a blue bucket hat. I had chucked this bucket hat in the bin so many times and he had taken it out and washed it. It wasn't a hat that he often wore. Normally a snap back and if the weather was bad, he went nowhere without his beanie hat on. He had pulled it down to cover his eyes from the sun as he slept. His phone began to ring which caused him to stir before eventually answering it. He only spoke a few words and then hung up. About 10 minutes later the phone rang again. He answered the phone,

"I'm coming to Croydon……", he paused.

"Nah I'm going to my aunts ……", he explained to whoever was on the other end of the phone.

"I don't think so……. Maybe later, I will shout you", he said as he hung up.

"Who was that?" I asked him

"Bradley", he said.

As we approached the Borough of Bromley his phone rang again.

"Yep, What Monks? Nah, I'm meant to go to my aunties, let me see if I can link you "Andre said.

He then turned to look at me. I had already heard the conversation so before he even had chance to say anything I replied "No!" He relayed that message to the person he was speaking to on the phone and then hung up. After another five minutes or so the phone rang again.

"I'm nearly there, coming into Bromley and up through Addington, let me ask her", he said

Andre turned to me and asked if I could drop him to Monks Hill to see his friend Bradley. As previously stated, I said "No". Again, he relayed the message.

"Where are you then?" Andre asked

"Okay so not far behind me, one sec" Andre turned to me and spoke.

"Mum, I know you don't want me to go to Monks, but I want to meet Bradley. Can you just drop me, and I will come straight to Aunties afterwards'?"

"No", I responded, becoming irritated.

"Okay cool" he said "Let's go Aunties and then I will just get the bus back"

I had real mixed emotions about that. I knew he would take himself from Upper Norwood to Monks Hill if he really wanted to and I didn't really want to allow him to do that.

"Can't you just come to Aunties and do what I am asking rather than go to the estate? You know I don't want you to go up there" I pleaded with him.

"I know Mum, but I haven't seen Bradley and them. I'm just going to link them, go studio quickly and then I will come back to Aunties, I promise"

We were on the Mad Mile, so I didn't have long to decide. We debated it back and forth until I decided that it was safer for me to drop Andre to meet his friend than for him to travel from one side of Croydon to the other on public transport. Why did this child always have a way of getting around me? If only he would listen sometimes, he would avoid some of the many troubles that he would find himself in.

As I approached the Monks Hill estate, the boys were all sat up and alert. It was so weird coming back onto the estate even though it had only been a matter of weeks. So much had happened in such a short space of time and although this felt like home it wasn't. I drove past our empty house and continued up to the back of the estate where the Spar food and wine shop was located. Andre and his friends often sat on the wall outside the shop, playing football, talking, and communicating with the residents on the estate. Everyone knew Andre, old and young. He was one of those kinds of people that others couldn't resist but to like and engage with.

Outside the Spar were the younger boys, Ashley's age. Normally Ashley would be playing football with them or arranging sleepovers or water fights which was normal for a hot summer evening. As we pulled up, Andre jumped out of the car. The sun was beaming from the sky and the local community was filled with the sounds of young people playing, people chatting and dogs barking. Teenagers kicking a football around and enjoying the summer sun.

"Where are you meeting Bradley?" I asked.

"He is five minutes away ", Andre replied

After deciding that he would leave his bag in the car and then changing his mind and grabbing it from the back so that he had his jumper with him he said goodbye to the boys and told me he loved me and would see me later.

"I'm letting you out with a heavy heart", I told him. He looked at me with a smile on his face.

"I love you mum", he said. "Don't worry I will be okay"

"Call me when you are ready to come to Aunties", I shouted as he crossed over the grass verge to the front of the shop.

I watched as the younger ones who were riding up and down on their bikes approached him with smiles on their faces. They loved Andre like a big brother and was always pleased to see him. He taught them football tricks, lectured them about school and the importance of getting an education and also chased them and engaged in playfighting activities. I looked at him stood there on the side of the road admiring how handsome he was. I half expected Ashley to want to get out of the car and insist that he should stay with his friends and Andre or at least for them to take a trip into the Spar to buy a drink or something. Neither of them did so with my surprise I told them to buckle up and we continued on our journey just a short fifteen minutes up the road to The Lawns.

As I drove off the estate in the flats in front of me, I could see two girls standing in the window of the stairwell.

"Is that Charlie?", I asked Ashley who had joined me to sit in the front passenger seat as Andre had got out.

Ashley confirmed that it was and as we drove closer to the flats, I could see her looking at us out of the window. Charlie had avoided us because most of the issues between Andre and the boys had begun since she had a relationship with Fabio. Andre and Charlie had been friends since we lived on the estate. When Charlie started dating Fabio all of them used to hang out together and over the space of a few months became very close. When Charlie's relationship with Fabio became toxic that is when troubles started between the group. Andre wasn't going to allow Fabio to beat up on Charlie and he became quite a protector. They continued to have a toxic on and off relationship but because of the violence Andre and Fabio's friendship ended abruptly. Even though Charlie had been at the core of the issues that we were facing, I didn't see her as a direct threat. She made silly decisions as a young lady, but I never had the impression that she was trying to cause problems. She had been caught up in teenage relationship issues and I just wished that she would sort herself out. I watched her as we approached and then once she was out of view, she was out of my mind, and we continued on our journey.

CHAPTER SEVEN
16TH AUGUST PART 2

I was hot and sticky and relieved that I had finally arrived at my destination. There were three flights of stairs to climb to get to Mandy's flat and after that drive I just couldn't imagine myself dragging overnight bags up the stairs. We jumped out, left the bags in the boot of the car, and made our way up. The house was cool. Mandy had the blinds drawn and the ceiling fan on as she sat on the sofa with her feet up watching Emmerdale. The room was bright and airy and soon became filled with hustle and bustle as we piled in. The phone which had no credit, and no data was my first priority. I searched for the internet password and connected my phone. After about two minutes my phone started to ring, it was WhatsApp. I didn't recognise the number or the picture that was being displayed but answered it, nevertheless. From the moment I answered the phone I knew that something was wrong. I had this feeling that swept over my body, and it made me feel uncomfortable. I got up from the table and moved into the hallway where my shoes were. I knew that I had to go somewhere.

"Yemi", I heard a panicked voice say.

I knew who it was. It was Natasha. Natasha was the mum of another one of Andre's friends. She also lived on the estate one street away from the Spar where I had dropped Andre earlier. It was unusual for Natasha to call me especially at this time, so my mind went into overdrive.

"What's happened Natasha?", I asked.

"Someone has been stabbed", she told me.

"What do you mean someone, who is it? Is it Andre?" I begged her down the phone.

I was already in the hallway pulling my shoes on. The boys could hear me and came to the doorway to see who I was talking too.

"I don't know" she said.

"Can you go and look?" I asked.

Natasha replied, "I don't want to, they are saying it is Andre".

"Can you see please Natasha?", I begged as I continued to put my shoes on and grab my car keys.

"Okay she said" and then she screamed. An almighty scream that I will never forget. Natasha loved Andre like a son. In fact, she called him Son.

I didn't need to hear anymore, I hung up the phone, shouted that Andre had been stabbed to my sister-in-law and headed out the front door. I didn't even wait to hear a response. If there was a response, I didn't hear it, I had only one thought on my mind and that was that I needed to get to my son as soon as I could. If I could have orbed there, I would have done just that.

The drive felt long. I couldn't get there quick enough. It seemed like every other car user on the road and every traffic light system or pedestrian that was waiting to cross the road were put there to slow my journey down. As I came off the roundabout at Gravel Hill, I felt close but still too far away. I actually didn't know where abouts Andre was, what I was going to see when I arrived or what the extent of his injuries were. I knew from Natasha's scream that it wasn't good, and I also knew that he hadn't called me to let me know that he was hurt or ok even. That wasn't a good sign because no matter what, he always called me first when he was ever in any kind of trouble.

I turned right into the estate; my heart was pounding in my chest. Turned left and glimpsed our old house. I was following in reverse the same route that I had taken a mere forty minutes ago. As I shot over the speed bumps in the road, I could see the end approaching. I had no idea what to expect. Would there be people around? Would he be sat on the wall after asking Natasha to call me? Would he be in a complete state, and I wouldn't be able to help him? Would there be Police and Paramedics there giving him treatment? My mind was contemplating a million different scenarios and each one made me feel scared.

As I turned right again my heart shot up into my mouth. In front of me on the grass was a bright red air ambulance. I had seen them in the sky but never this close. Seeing this helicopter put me into complete panic mode. The road on the left had Police tape blocking it off. Heather Way, the road that his friend lived on, the mum who had called me to come. I turned into the road and slammed on my brakes as the Police tape hit my window screen. I jumped out of the car with my heart racing and without even shutting the door, I started to run.

The road felt silent, everything happening in slow motion. In front of me on the grass in front of a block of flats I could see people. Lots of them. As I ran the length of the street, I watched them turning to look at me one at a time. It was all happening so slowly.

"It's his mum" I could hear people saying. "He was calling for her"

Through the crowds I was searching for a glimpse of my son. Just a tiny glimpse to let me know how he was. As I continued to run towards the gathered people, two Police officers began approaching me from out of the crowd. I didn't slow down but they broke my stride as they stopped me in the street. I didn't need to tell them who I was, they just knew.

"Where is my son?", I demanded. They didn't want me to get any closer, I could tell that from the way they were behaving.

"They are doing everything that they can to help him", the female officer said.

"I need to go to him", I said

"No", was the response. I wasn't allowed to go to my son at a time that he needed me the most. He was calling for his mum after all, it was me that he wanted. The female Police officer explained to me that they were giving him emergency care and that it was best that I waited and let them do their jobs, so I agreed to stand back. I spun around and there were people everywhere looking at me. Some were hugging each other. Some were crying and others were standing looking very spaced out. As I stood in the middle of the street watching the people watching me, I noticed Bradley sitting on the wall. I recognised quite a few people that were there, but there were also others who I didn't know. I cast my eyes onto him, looked away and then back at him. No one approached me. No one had come forward to tell me what was going on. I felt numb but I had a funny feeling take over my body. I stated to walk towards Bradley and the expression that he had on his face made me feel uneasy. I instantly felt that I was no longer amongst friends, amongst people that I knew and trusted. There was a dark feeling in the air.

"You did this", I said to him.

Bradley looked at me, but no words came out of his mouth.

"Did you hear what I said?" I questioned him again. "You did this to my son" I shouted.

He stood up and started to approach me with a look of confusion on his face.

"If anything happens to Andre, I am going to hold you responsible", I told him.

"Yemi", I heard a voice call me and as I spun around my brother-in-law and my niece were standing there.

My sister met Ray when Andre was about two years old. I think Ray, at the time, couldn't believe how hyperactive Andre was for a young boy. Andre used to jump all over him and irritate him so much. As Andre grew up and began playing football his relationship with Ray changed. They joked around together and Ray would often tell him that he was his favourite nephew. Anytime Andre found himself in a problematic situation he would get advice from Uncle Ray. I knew Ray would take the situation into hand and get the answers that were needed at the time because he was that type of man.

Stood next to Ray was my niece Jadine. Jadine and Andre were eighteen months apart in age. My eldest sisters first child and my mums first grandchild. They were very close too. When they were little, and my sister first went back to work I looked after them both. I would take Jadine to Playschool and spend my days caring for them both. Yes, they drove me crazy at times and together they would get up to all sorts of mischief. I had put them both down for a nap one day and after twenty minutes of listening to messing about and then silence, I went to check on them to see if they had finally fallen asleep. Both were covered from head to foot in thick greasy eczema cream. Not only had they covered themselves, but they had also decided to rub it into the nicely painted nursery wall. It took such a long to clean the cream off the wall and both of them, but that was nothing compared to the time that I found them both stood in the toilet bowl, feet soaking wet, hiding from me.

All three of us stood there not knowing the extent of injuries Andre had sustained. I was hanging onto every sight and every sound hoping for something that would give me some hope that he would be alright. All we could do is watch as the back of the ambulance doors reopened, and a red blanket shield was erected around him. There were lots of movements from Paramedics and Police. Through the gap I could see his skin. He was laying on an ambulance trolley, but my vision was blocked by the movement. After a short while the ambulance doors were shut again and Jadine and I were taken to a Police car.

"They have had to open up Andre's chest", the male Policeman explained." He is going to be taken by road to St George's Hospital, I will drive you if you want to get in the back"

I handed Ray my car keys and after a brief conversation where he explained that he would be going back home to get my sister and meet us there, he left.

Jadine and I got into the back of the Police car, and we followed in convoy enroute to the hospital. The ambulance was in front with their sirens and blue lights going and the car I was travelling in was doing exactly the same thing. The officer had his radio low, and I think this is so that we couldn't hear from the back of the car what was happening. We had travelled a short way and all of a sudden, my chest went tight, and I was struggling to breath. I looked up and through the blinds at the back of the ambulance I could see the Paramedics in what I can only describe as a panicked state. I felt as if the life was being sucked out of my body. Jadine looked worried as she tried to help me. It passed and I calmed back down. This happened twice on the journey to the hospital, and I honestly felt that I was going to die on the way. It wasn't until later down the line that I understood why. As we approached the hospital the Police car slowed down as the ambulance sped ahead. We circled a few times before the car pulled up and let me out. There was the ambulance that my injured son had travelled in, the doors wide open but Andre was nowhere to be seen. I instantly knew that this was a deliberate move to ensure that I didn't see him or come into contact with him. I needed to see my son. I had always been there for him, to hold his hand no matter what. There was only one occasion that I could think of when Andre was injured, and I hadn't been there, and this was when he was about eleven months old.

I had been to a talent show with my friend and Andre had stayed with my eldest sister Lorraine, Jadine's mum. After an evening of them both adding unsavoury designs to my sister's hair and clipping in an array of colourful bobbles and clips, they went on to play toddler chase around the solid pine coffee table. A couple of rotations around the table and being told to slow down and stop, Andre tripped on the edge of the rug stationed beneath the coffee table, and as he fell caught his eye on the corner of the table. Needless to say, my sister spent the evening in A&E whilst he had his eyebrow stitched up, still with the more than amusing hair style. The next morning when she brought him home, I could do nothing but lay on the floor as I felt physically sick from knowing that he was in pain and guilty that I had not been there when he needed me.

Andre was clumsy. I think it was because of his agility and daring personality. He had slid across the floor and bashed the door frame resulting in a massive sized coco on his forehead. He had dragged his feet over the door bar and sliced the skin off the top of his toe. Not to mention when he climbed the neighbour's apple tree only to fall through the bushes scrapping his chest area. More recently he had slipped on the pavement outside the supermarket and cracked his knee cap. Andre spent three days limping around before showing me his injury by which time looked like he had an oversized tennis ball sticking out of his rather skinny knee. A trip to A&E and a full leg cast later meant that for the first time in his life since he had the ability to walk, he had to sit still. This didn't last long. After falling down the stairs and a trip up the road to the shop on crutches, which tested his upper body strength, Andre decided it wasn't for him and in the night, he used scissors to cut off the cast which I fell over in the morning when I went to check on him.

I rushed into the hospital and stood in front of the locked doors to Resus. In front of these doors stood an armed Police Officer. I was shown the waiting room and told that I would be given an update shortly. What was I supposed to do, just sit, and wait? I'm not sure how but people started to arrive at the hospital. My Mum and Sisters arrived. My sister-in-law, my brother-in-law and Andre's dad. I called my husband, and he made his way to be with the children who had been taken to my eldest sister's house to be with their cousins. We sat in the waiting room for what seemed like ages with no news. No news is good news, right? We talked, we prayed, we begged for someone to keep him safe. Times and timing during this period are not something that I can even pretend to remember. We were all hoping to hear that our little fighter was okay. I walked in and out of that building not knowing what to do with myself. I just needed to hear some news, something to give me some hope. I have never felt so useless in all my life, a mother is supposed to protect her children and there was nothing that I could do right now but put my faith in the professionals to bring my child back home to me.

Finally, a female doctor appeared at the doorway. She asked us all to join her in another waiting room so that she could talk to us about what happened to Andre. We all crammed into the tiny room. Some were sat down, others were stood. We were all in different states of mind. I was numb, not shed a tear, trying to hold it all together and be strong.

"I don't know if you know what injuries Andre sustained tonight", the doctor said. We all continued to stare at her waiting for news.

"Andre received injuries to.......", she continued, and as I became impatient, I jumped in.

"Is he dead?", I asked with agony in my voice.

"Unfortunately........."

I didn't hear any more of what the doctor said. At this moment I knew that my son had died, and the internal pain hit me like someone had just shot me with a thousand bullets. I could feel my legs trembling and although I wanted to run, I couldn't move. I fell from an upright position and hit the floor with a bang. I wailed and I wailed, and I wailed. A sound was pouring out of my body that I can never describe. I could feel my heart hitting the floor as it beat rapidly. I went into an overwhelming state of shock and total loss of emotional control. I couldn't believe what the doctor had just told me.

I could hear nothing; all I could feel was the cold floor beneath me and I didn't want to get up. It was the pain from my teeth and nose that I had smashed on the floor as I hit the ground that brought me round. I pulled myself to my feet. My face was soaked with tears and my vision blurry. I felt as if I was trapped inside a ball of clear smoke that was clouding my vision and blocking out all the sound. I noticed that everyone in the room was sobbing. My mum was sobbing uncontrollably, my sisters, my nieces but I couldn't hear them. I needed air; my brain was scrambling up I did not know if what I had been told was true. I was confused. Why would my son be dead? What happened to him? Who did this to my baby? I needed answers but none were coming.

I ran outside looking for someone, anyone that could help me to make sense of the information that I had just been given. There was no one there. I went to the door and banged furiously hoping that someone would let me in, or I would see Andre in the distance, but the doors wouldn't open. I ran outside, I needed fresh air, I kicked over a bin and slumped myself on the floor of the entrance. As I sat there in a state of shock with my head in my hands sobbing, I struggled to get my breathing to normalise. My phone was ringing. I stared at the screen for a short while before answering it. The voice at the other end of the phone said,

"How's your boy"

"Dead", I replied, and hung up.

CHAPTER EIGHT
THE MORNING AFTER THE NIGHT BEFORE

I still, until this day, cannot describe how I felt that night at the hospital. The night was long. I had to absorb that my first-born son had been murdered, that he was dead, and process that I would never see his face smiling back at me again. After I went from being in an erratically emotional state from the initial shock of the news, I quickly turned to numbness as the disbelief set in. How could any of this be true? I went over all the steps we took that evening, and nothing about what occurred made sense to me.

It is very different when someone you know becomes ill or old. You know your loved one will eventually pass away, and with this knowledge, you have an opportunity to come to terms with living without them. Although it hurts, your brain can process how you feel when the time comes, and the grieving process can begin instantly. When someone you love is young and healthy, and you see them a few hours before, being told they are dead is difficult to process and come to terms with.

The year previously, I lost a very close friend of mine. Another mother from The Lawns family. Sam and I had been friends since I were about nineteen years old. Even though we had our ups and downs, fallouts, and make-ups, we were still extremely close. My children adored Sam; Andre especially had been very close to her. In fact, he called her mum. Sam had been diagnosed with cancer, and on her last visit to the hospital, she had been given the news that she only had three weeks to live. The announcement was devastating and took everyone by complete surprise. In those remaining weeks, we had the opportunity to build all bridges and just talk through many situations that we had not previously had the opportunity to discuss. When Sam finally passed away, I could grieve almost immediately because I knew the day was coming soon and I had prepared myself mentally for when it eventually came. I went home that night and cried deeply for her. Andre was extremely devastated, so much so that he wouldn't even consider attending her funeral.

"My Aunty is 43 years old; why am I going to a funeral for someone so young? It doesn't make sense", he told me.

It didn't matter how much I tried to convince Andre to come; he refused. At that point in my life, I did not think that I would go through an even more unbearable loss than I faced the day that Samantha died. Now I had lost Andre and I didn't know how to respond to this news, was I supposed to accept that my child had died and just start the grieving process like I did a year ago for my friend. As I sat in the hospital feeling disoriented, patiently waiting for the time to come, which they had promised me would be very soon to see my son, I prayed for Sam to collect him. The thought of losing him and for his spirit to be out there somewhere on his own was killing me and the small piece of comfort I held onto at that time was knowing that they would now be together.

It didn't take long before the realisation that the information I was given by the police that I would be able to see my son was untrue. The police officer that had been guarding the room, came out to inform me that Andre's body was now being classed as evidence and that nobody, not even me, would be able to see him. The Officer stated that it was being viewed as a live investigation and they couldn't risk tampering with that. Hearing this type of information was devastating. That was my child that they were talking about. He's not a piece of evidence just to be laid out on a cold slab for you to prod around with and get evidence from. That's my baby; surely, I had a right to see him. I didn't even know what injuries he had. Had he been stabbed once or twice, where were those injuries on his body. What had these people done to him that was so bad it resulted in the ending of his life. I desperately tried to argue my point with them, but here was nothing more that I could do, the decision had been made. Nobody knew what else to do. We couldn't remain at the hospital all night; we weren't going to be able to see Andre and we all had children at home who we still hadn't broken the news to. Plans for the night were discussed and then everybody except Mandy and I left the hospital and made their way home.

It was 11:30 at night, and the time seemed to just be flying past. I'd spoken to my husband, and we had decided that he should break the news to the boys once my sister Lorraine and her husband returned home. Ashley was already asking questions because the newspapers had already started to report that Andre had died and were keeping a live coverage of the event going. Ashley was getting angry at people who were posting, and he was telling them that I hadn't told him or confirmed that Andre died so that they must all just be quiet and wait until I had spoken. But I couldn't. I could not bear to look at my children and tell them their big brother had died and that is why I had left that task to the others to do. Once they had all gone, I had stayed at the hospital to talk to the police and give them any information I had to help them work out what happened and who caused this. Everyone who left the hospital that night was in disbelief, extremely upset and unable to put how they were feeling into words. They were heartbroken for themselves, but they were also heartbroken for the children and for me.

The police officer who I had to speak to before I left was called Katy, she introduced herself as being our family liaison officer or FLO for short. Katy would be there to support me through the whole process. Tonight, her purpose was to gather as much useful information from me as possible and find out if there was any background history or issues that could have led to this horrendous tragedy on this night. Because of the build-up, I was adamant in my mind that I knew who was responsible for my son's death. I gave her a full breakdown of all the incidents that had occurred previously and the names, addresses, schools, and any other information that I could think of that would help them locate them quickly. Katy also asked me to give over any phone numbers I had for Andre and any of his friends. As I went into my phone to retrieve the phone numbers, I realised I had countless numbers saved for Andre. They were named Andre, Andre one, Dee, and Drose. I gave them all to her because at the time, I couldn't even remember which one of those numbers I used to ring him most recently.

Katy explained to me the process that would happen over the next few days, including identifying Andre's body. I couldn't even think that far ahead, my brain felt so heavy, and my body was exhausted from all the pain that I was carrying. In the blink of an eye, my world had come tumbling down. I was in a hospital 45 miles away from the place I now called home. I had one dead child, two children that needed me who I couldn't bear to see, and just a couple of overnight items that I had thrown into a bag for my trip back down to Croydon. My life had fallen apart, and I didn't know where to start making sense of it or putting any of the pieces back together. In hindsight, I should probably have gone back to my sisters that night to be with the boys, which I think about often. At the time, I could not deal with anybody else's grief. Watching everyone else's pain was tearing me apart.

I didn't know how I was feeling or how to respond to the day's events. I actually didn't want my children to see me in that state. I had always been the strong parent who could give them the advice they needed and to be there for them when things were going bad. To be the one to tell them everything would be okay. To ask them not to worry because I would sort it all out. This was the first time in my life that I didn't have the answers. I couldn't tell them everything was going to be okay, and I definitely couldn't put everything right. As a mother, I felt like a failure; how did I fail at keeping my son safe? I started to blame myself. Had I not dropped Andre off and just forced him to come straight with me to Auntie Mandy's then maybe he would still be sitting here right now, or would he still have been in that room laying on a cold slab, gone?

It's so easy to judge and be hard on yourself. The feeling of loss of control is detrimental and I think that I needed that time alone to process what was going on. Knowing that my husband was with the boys, that my sister and her husband and her children were there also made it easier for me to just take that time that I needed. I needed space to think about everything that had happened, process my thoughts and my feelings, so I went to my sister-in-law's house back on The Lawns, where I spent the whole night sitting on a stool in her kitchen waiting for the sun to rise.

As soon as it reached 6:00 AM, my thoughts moved to informing my family members who may not already be aware. My uncle Kevin was the first person on my list of people to call. He loved Andre, and Andre loved him. My Uncle would call him Fred; that was his nickname. We'd spent a lovely summer evening at my uncle Kevin's a few weeks before all the incidents unfolded. Again, this was a funny day because typically, two children were always missing from gatherings when the family got together. Jadine was one of them; she very rarely made an appearance at any type of social gathering our family had, and Andre was the other. On this day, both showed up, and the shenanigans that we all got up to in my uncle's garden are memories that I will never forget and hold dear to me for as long as I live.

My cousin who is a few months younger than me decided on that day that he would continue to play the game of 'one up' with me that we had been playing for years and would commence anytime we were together. My Uncle and Aunts Garden felt enchanted, and the children loved the time that they spent there, feeding the fish, and admiring the beautiful array of flowers that were growing. On this particular day there was a bouncy castle inflated on the grass to keep the younger ones entertained and a rather large paddling pool on the middle of the lawn. My cousin decided to arm all the children with water pistols and so the annoying process of filling and squirting all the adults began. As usual Andre and my cousin Barry together couldn't behave themselves and needless to say they soon hatched a plan to get 'one up' on me. A bucket of water later, which landed over my head, I then took to bum shoving my cousin into the pool. Everyone was soaked through and luckily for us it was a hot sunny day, so we were able to dry off somewhat before heading home. I dialled my uncle's number, and it rang for a short while before my other cousin answered the phone.

"Gemma, is your dad up?" I asked.

As my cousin went to call her dad, I was frantically rehearsing in my head what I was going to say. I was exhausted from crying and lack of sleep but as she went to call him, I started to deep breath in order to hold back further tears. It was strange for me to call their home so early in the morning, so I think Uncle Kevin knew before he even came to the phone that something wrong was up.

"Uncle Kevin", I said, trying to hold back the tears.

"I wanted to call you before you switched the television on or looked at a newspaper this morning. Andre was murdered last night", and with that, I burst into tears.

I don't know what my uncle said. I can't remember the response he gave. But I know that they were all devastated and later that day they came to find me.

I made a few more calls that morning. I made a call to my friend and work colleague to let her know what had happened. Her mum was the Deputy Head at the school I worked at, so I knew that she would pass the message on to them, so they were all aware. I called a few more family members and friends as the news had started to spread so fast on the television, newspapers, and social media. Andre was being named as the eighth teenager to be murdered in the capital that year, so at the time, knife related incidents which resulted in murder were still pretty rare. What annoyed me most was the total disregard for the feelings of the family. Because of the constant updates on social media from the local papers it made it near on impossible to keep my children from finding out that their brother had died before my sister and husband had reached home. When the boys were eventually told that night, both had broken down instantly in tears. I was told that the scream that Ashley gave out was heart wrenching. As selfish as it may seem, I am glad that I never witnessed it because I think that it would have finished me off.

My next priority for the day was to make my way back to my sister's house to be with the boys. I was nervous about seeing them because I didn't know if I was strong enough to deal with their grief on top of mine. Mandy drove me there as I had abandoned my own car the day before when I jumped in the back of the Police car to follow the ambulance. Ray had taken the car back to their home but insisted that my sister didn't drive it because we looked so alike, and nobody knew at the time if there was a risk to anymore of us. In the boot of the car were our bags, the Xbox and TV monitor that the boys had brought with to keep them entertained on the trip. As soon as I arrived, I climbed into the car and sat with my hand on the passenger seat. Andre had been sat there so peaceful hours before, I could feel him still there and as I rubbed the seat with my hand, I let out a gut-wrenching scream.

It was the saddest day I've ever experienced in my whole entire life. Once seeing the boys, we all hugged and cried together and then sat holding each other on the sofa. I didn't know whether to cry or just curl up in a ball and go to sleep for as long as needed but I knew that they both needed me, and I never stayed away from them again after that. There were so many of us at my sister's that it was overwhelming. I felt like I was on show; everybody was looking to me to see how I would react and to be there to support me should I break. For some reason, I just couldn't let my tears go. It was probably because I had so many things to do. I had to ensure that those responsible for taking my son's life were brought to justice. I needed to ensure that my children were okay and support them as best I could. I needed to make sure my mum was alright. Andre was her first-born grandson, who she adored, and I could see that she didn't know how to deal with the grief and the pain that she was feeling, let alone have the strength to support me, her daughter.

Nobody knew what to say to each other, so most of the time, we just tried to keep busy with nonsense activities, and for the most time we scrolled through the Internet to see what people were saying or what the newspapers had written. Later that afternoon, a few of us decided that we should go to the area on Heather way, where Andre had been murdered the night before. When we arrived, an overwhelming number of people were at the scene. The police tape was still in place, and against the lamp post in the middle of the crime scene were those red blankets that had been used to shield him whilst the paramedics fought to save his life. I was in disbelief that nobody had cleaned those blankets away instead of leaving them there at the crime scene for us all to see. Looking at the aftermath made me want to vomit. The night before we did not know the extent of injuries and today as we stood there, we knew that it resulted in his life being over.

The number of young people sitting on the wall on the corner of Heather Way was unbelievable. I had people approaching me, hugging me, and sending their condolences. Some I knew and some I had never met before. They brought flowers, candles, tea lights, and other items to lay down in memory of their friend Andre. On the grass verge I could see a dark patch. It caught my eye because of the shape and where it was. I stared into the space for a while before shaking myself out of the torment that it was causing. I knew it was his blood, but there was just so much.

As the night began to get dark, a man approached me with his daughter. Everyone seemed to know who I was. He handed me a huge bunch of lilies and a card of condolences. He explained he had already laid flowers for Andre, and that this bunch was for me. He told me that he had put something inside the card to help, so asked me not to put it down or lose it. I thanked him before we talked about how he knew my son. The man was a father of a daughter who had been friends with Andre. He explained how gentlemanly and caring my son was and how he had been so protective over his daughters. He went on to explain that in the evenings, when they were on the estate hanging out in the park, Andre would always make sure that the girls got home safe, even if he had to walk them back alone before returning home himself. He said how impressed he was with his caring nature and how he appreciated the way that he treated his daughters. This may sound extremely strange because although I knew Andre inside out and back to front, I was now learning first-hand from others just how loving and kind he really was. Not just to me but to his brothers, extended family, and friends and members of the community. He was the most caring young man I'd ever met, and it may sound as if I am saying this because he's my son, but he generally was. Hearing the testimonies from this man and others who had approached me that evening confirmed my own feelings and opinions of him and made me feel so proud.

As I stood on the side of the road, my phone began to ring. It was a private number, so I answered it quickly. The first time that I'd spoken to my family liaison officer since the night before. She was calling me to update me on the investigation and what they had pieced together so far. She informed me that three of the four suspects they had been looking for had been arrested and were currently in custody. My heart jumped when I heard the news and I took a huge sigh of relief knowing that they were in custody. I asked her the names of those who had been arrested so she called them out to me. I made a mental check of whether they were the ones I had suspected of being part of this vicious attack on my son. The first person who was arrested was Fabio. This matched my suspicions as I believed from the moment, I heard that Andre had been stabbed, that this young man had significant involvement in his murder. The second person arrested was called Jamell. I didn't know this name; this wasn't a name that was familiar to me, and I didn't have any idea of the part that he could have played in this or why. The third person who had been identified to me that evening was named Rodney. I also didn't know who this person was, but after speaking to Andre's friends and the young people, it was revealed that he went by the nickname Glare, which is a name that I was familiar with. He was the one that I had heard the boys talking about in the garden the morning after the shooting. I had no idea who the fourth person was that they were looking for. There was a name of another young man who I thought was involved, all I could do is continue to wait until that person was caught and name confirmed. Hearing this kind of information is bittersweet. Even though I felt relieved that people had actually been arrested on suspicion of the murder of my son, the pain was still deep that I'd lost him. The need for justice starts to take over; getting those crucial answers about what happened and why is only the start of that process.

Watching the young people spell Andre's name out in tea lights on the grass made me silently weep. All his usual friends such as Bradley, Alex and Mark were there. Andre's first love was there, and many other friends arrived to show their support for us as a family and for one another as they all mourned the loss of their dear friend. Young people are funny at a time when somebody is taken away in such tragic circumstances. I found that young people behaved strangely. There were very little tears, but you could see the sadness on their faces. I would observe their behaviour as they interacted with each other, hugging, and sitting in deep thought. Not knowing what to do or say but acting out an array of actions that represented their loss and how they were feeling. They played music from their cars, deafening songs that evoked sad emotion. They participated in drinking alcohol and smoking cannabis. They bought tee shirts and teddy bears and candles with messages attached to them simply saying 'RIP Bro', and a whole array of other items to place at the area where he was stabbed. After watching the movements of the young people, I decided that enough was enough for one night, and I needed to go home. But I had no home. I couldn't imagine ever returning to the house in Gillingham, so I went back to my sisters with the boys, where we made the best of a bad situation and created sleeping spaces for myself, my husband who stayed to support us all, and the children on the living room floor.

I couldn't sleep that night; as I lay there staring at the ceiling, my eyes began to fill with tears. The past two days had been like a whirlpool; one minute, I was swimming around at the top with loads of room to breathe, and all of a sudden, I was being sucked deeper and deeper below the surface, down to a very dark place where I found myself suffocating. In those quiet moments, in the middle of the night, you begin to reflect on the tragedy that has unfolded in front of your eyes. I still had this feeling of losing control, knowing that Andre was dead but not knowing how it happened with every detail. When it came to my children, I always insisted on knowing everything. This had also been mine and Andre's code of honour to one another; I always told him that I need to know the truth no matter what, good, bad, ugly or if it hurt me. It's in those moments of truth and honesty that you can really reflect and make informed decisions about what to do next. I hated that it was a police investigation; it felt as if something that belonged to me, this loving, beautiful boy that I had brought into the world, was now just a piece of evidence. I just didn't know how I would continue to live without him, and that thought erupted pain from my stomach all the way up into my chest and planted itself deeply in my throat.

What else could I have done to just sort out the issues that I knew he was having with these boys. It was always tricky because Andre would always play situations down. Because of his calm persona and the way, he dealt with things he always tried to see the best in people at the worst times. However, what was happening to us at the Heathfield house had become scary, out of control and unmanageable and that definitely wasn't how I wanted to live. Andre never really gave off a sense that he thought he was in any real danger. Throughout this entire situation, Andre never once displayed fear; if he had, I think I would have been in a more emotionally heightened state in the earlier days.

The sun started to rise; it was around 5:00 AM, and I still hadn't closed my eyes to sleep. I actually hadn't slept since Monday night. I had woken up on that Tuesday morning, and by that evening, my whole life had turned upside down. I hadn't slept Tuesday night Or Wednesday night, and now it was Thursday morning. All of a sudden, in your life, you have nothing else to do but sit and wait for someone to tell you what is happening next; I had so many questions to ask, so today was going to be the day to get some answers. When it reached 9:00 AM, I made my first phone call to Katy, the FLO. I needed to get an update on what was happening and agreed to meet her at The Lawns. After watching my sister hanging washing out in the garden whilst I smoked and drank coffee, I got ready and made my way there. I didn't want to take the children because I did not want them to overhear any conversations regarding what happened to their brother.

It was bad enough that there had been videos posted online on the metro newspaper website, a video of the paramedics and the police fighting to save Andre as he lay face down on the grass verge surrounded by lots of people. I watched that video and it was painful to view. I could see the air ambulance circulating in the air and another lady who was kneeling down beside him. There were Police and paramedics, and Andre was laying topless covered by an aluminium blanket. He looked so petite, slim, and lifeless. I was angry that this had been shared. I spoke to the man who had made that video, and he told me that he'd made it to help the police in their investigations. He asked me if I wanted to see it, and I declined; he asked me what I wanted him to do with the video, and I responded to delete it. How it went from being deleted to online for everybody to watch and comment about, I just don't know. It's tough to understand what goes through people's heads when they do such things; do they not think about the implications that it will have on families.

It made me think about Andre and how private he was on his social media. Andre wasn't one to publicly post or share pictures of himself. I made the decision there and then that I would try and honour him and the way he viewed social media by keeping as much about his image as private as could be.

CHAPTER NINE
INVESTIGATIONS AND ARRESTS

I made my way to my sister-in-laws and waited for Katy to arrive. She was a lovely lady, so caring, considerate, and understanding, but you could tell she was a police officer just from how she carried herself. Very quickly I came to trust her, and I knew almost straightaway she would be somebody I would be able to speak to and rely on throughout the investigation.

"Hi, Yemi," she said as she bundled through the door carrying a handbag over her left arm and holding other pieces of paperwork seen poking out of multi-coloured folders.

Katy clearly had things that she needed to discuss with me today and I was all ears. There had been so many versions of events from that night that people were discussing, but I needed clarity from Police about what was true and what was exaggerated.

"So, we've made three arrests. They are currently being held at the police station. We have applied for their hold time to be extended so that we can continue questioning them before a decision is made whether to charge or release," Katy told me.

Katy informed me that they were still looking for one more suspect, but they were finding it difficult to locate him and information suggested that he was on the run. They had received so much intelligence from members of the public who had witnessed Andre's murder and they were continuing to follow up on leads. It was a delicate situation because I was able to give so much information and was therefore a key witness. Should the case go to trial it was more than likely that I would be called to the stand. Because of this, the amount of information that was being given to me was restricted. I understood but couldn't help but to feel frustrated.

"Have you been back to the house in Kent since this happened?" Katy asked me.

"No, why?" I replied

"This might sound like a bit of a weird request, but we will need to go there now as I have to check if any of the knives we've recovered, match any you have at your home."

I started to laugh, and Katy looked at me as if I was mad.

"None of the knives you have recovered are going to match anything I've got at my house," I assured her.

Katy had probably heard this before, it was her job after all, but I was one hundred per cent certain she wouldn't find what she was looking for. Katy looked at me; she was probably wondering how I could be so confident with what I said but there was a good reason. I only had three knives in my house, two identical vegetable knives with small sleeves that covered the blades and a bread knife. Each knife was no bigger than the size of your hand. My family and friends used to laugh at me when in my kitchen wanting to cut something. The knives I owned did everything I needed them to do, so I didn't see the need to have any wild and wonderful knife block sets that just sat on the side looking attractive.

Honestly, I wanted to remove any temptation that there would ever be for one of my three sons or any of their friends to pick up a knife and carry it outside with them. I made that decision quite early on in Andre's teenage years. I knew someone whose son had been murdered in Norbury a good few years ago, and I remember the feeling of dread when I heard the news. I remember trying to imagine how the boys mum had been coping and how his death must have impacted their family. Two years before, my son's cousin had also been stabbed in his heart in Croydon, again that was a horrific time to watch how his mum and family dealt with his loss. That was the first funeral that Ashley attended and now he was going to have to go through it once again but for his own brother. More recently, there had been a knife attack in Selsdon, not far from where we lived, we got up one morning to find that Police had cordoned off Addington Road. I remember trying to protect the children from knowing what had occurred because it appeared to be a random attack where the man was stabbed one hundred times. I took the responsibility to be accountable for any knives kept in my home. If I had more than three, it was too many; I just kept the bare minimum of what I needed, and that's how I liked it.

"Do we need to go right now?" I asked her in an uncomfortable way.

This was going to be an arduous journey for me. I hadn't returned to the house since the morning that we all left together; I wasn't quite sure if I was ready for that. Katy explained that it was best to get it over and done with and that once we arrived, she would lead me. Maybe she thought I would try to remove or hide things that I didn't want her to see. I had nothing to hide, and she was more than welcome to come to the house and look for herself. I agreed, and we jumped into her car, ready to go.

When we arrived at the house and I opened the back door, my stomach went up in my mouth. I felt really uneasy about going back inside and I could feel my body trembling. So many memories of that last day together and now I felt extremely sad recalling any of it. I was questioning whether I had made the correct choice to move from Croydon to Kent in the first place. Should I have just stayed in our home, where we were familiar, where we had people around us, where Andre could have run too and come straight in if he needed to at any time? I should have stood up and made the Police listen to what I was telling them about the three incidents before this murder. I should have pushed for more support and maybe gone to Fabio's house to speak to his parents. Stepping back into that house, into a place that I was trying to make home for at least three weeks, was hard. I wanted to blame everyone around me; the neighbours for complaining and making me feel that I needed to leave. The landlord for reading me the riot act and Police for not having those conversations that I thought that they would automatically do. All I could do was blame myself, Andre, and everyone else who contributed to the decision making in the lead up to Andre's murder; but really the only people who could be blamed were those who committed the crime.

"Where do you keep the knives?" Katy asked.

I walked into the kitchen, which I actually loved so much more than the kitchen at the Heathfield house. Everything was integrated, so you could not see where the fridge, dishwasher or the washing machine were kept. It was all hidden behind wooden cupboard doors.

"It's that one," I said as I pointed at the cupboard nearest the sink in the corner.

The dishwasher is where all the knives should be at this point. As I thought about the meal Andre had prepared for us before we left for Croydon that day, I suddenly had this overwhelming feeling of dread. I had this thought stuck in my head that I couldn't shift; I could only picture the Last Supper from the Bible. Things about that day just didn't feel normal to me. It was as though Andre knew that this could possibly be his last day on earth, and he had done an array of out-of-the-ordinary things as a gesture before he left. That was the first time in a long time since we all sat down at a table and ate together, and he made that happen. Just by rustling up all the leftover food in the fridge, preparing it, and laying it out on the table, we all had that last opportunity to sit together as we ate, talked, and laughed as a family. As thoughts of that day began to take over my mind, I became overwhelmed and made this peculiar noise as I tried to muffle the sob about to leave my body. As Katy opened the cupboard door, the front of the dishwasher, this almighty odour flew out and filled the room.

"Oh my gosh", I said as I looked at the over-full dishwasher, embarrassed and trying to work out why it had been left like that.

It was full of every single plate, cup, knife, fork, spoon, and pot you could imagine. Thinking back to the events of the day I remembered that as we rushed around trying to pack our belongings to take, I had asked Andre to turn on the dishwasher. He grabbed the dishwasher tablet put it into the drawer and shut the door but hadn't turned it on properly. If he was here now, I would have been shouting at him. You had to love Andre. As great as he was in the kitchen, the oven was probably the only appliance he could ever navigate. He clearly didn't know how to put the dishwasher on, which is why the pots and plates were sat there for days rotting and covered in mould and smelling out the entire kitchen. He had the same problem with the washing machine.

A few months before leaving Heathfield, we had a new washing machine that we hadn't had a chance to plumb into the kitchen; it was one of those jobs that my husband was going to get around to doing but hadn't actually done yet. It wasn't a secret. Everybody knew that the washing machine wasn't plumbed in. Still, on this particular day, as I got home from work and stood on the doorstep looking at the door, I sensed something was wrong. As I pushed the front door open, the water started to run out, over the doorstep and down the front path; it was about three centimetres thick in every downstairs room. It continued making its way slowly outside as I called Andre to see where he was; I didn't get a response, so after further screaming and hollering up the stairs, finally, he appeared half asleep on the top of the stairway.

"What are you doing?" I asked him.

I don't even know why I bothered to ask. The child had put on the washing machine, left the pipe hanging on the floor, went upstairs, and fallen asleep. As a result, the washing machine had done a whole hour wash cycle and pumped all the wastewater from inside the machine over the kitchen floor. There we all were, me, my husband and even the two younger children using every single towel, sheet, and cloth that we could find to soak the water up and squeeze it out in the back garden. It took us about two hours to clean up all the water. Needless to say, Andre never touched that washing machine again.

After the horror of the dishwasher, Katy moved on to look inside the drawers. She opened the drawer and found the tiny little red knife. Katy put it down on the side and then discreetly tried to pull some paperwork from her briefcase. I couldn't see clearly what was on the paper, but it was a photograph. I got a glimpse of what looked like a red-handled kitchen knife, and she was comparing it to the kitchen knife she had just taken out of my kitchen drawer. After a quick comparison, Katy returned the knife to the drawer before she turned around to look at me.

"I know you said you only had three knives, and I've only found three, but are you sure that's it?"

"Yep", I replied as she pushed the papers back into her folder.

"I wonder if I could go up now and search Andre's room, if possible," she asked me still trying to keep an air of respect for me and what I was going through.

"Yes, of course, you can", I said as I began directing her through the living room and up the stairs.

We went upstairs, and she pushed open the bedroom door. I couldn't bring myself to go inside the room. I don't know why it just didn't feel right. Andre wasn't there and would never come back, and I just didn't think at that point that I wanted to be in the same room where his belongings were. I watched as Katy entered the room. She stood still for a moment and then moved further inside so she could see around his tiny little box bedroom. We had spoken about Andre's room in the car on the drive to the house. I told her that Andre didn't have anything in his bedroom. By using the word anything, Katy had thought that I had meant anything that might incriminate him. I actually meant anything at all. Andre was a funny person; he wasn't a keeper of possessions. In fact, he didn't own much at all. Not because he couldn't possess much but because he just lived a simple life. From a very young age, Andre amazed me with his minimalistic lifestyle. He never asked for anything; that child owned one pair of trainers, and he would wear them until his toe was poking out the bottom. I would then buy him new shoes, and he wouldn't want to wear them because they weren't comfortable, and he preferred the old ones, and he would continue to go to school every day with the holey shoes, embarrassing me in the playground in front of the other parents. It would probably take about a week of fighting him until, in the end, I would have to force him to wear the shoes.

One day, I think Andre was in Year Four, as I pulled up outside the school, Andre had the new Astro turf trainers on his feet.

"Go on, then off you go". I said to him.

Andre got out of the car, grabbed his rucksack, looked inside, and realised that the trainers with the hole were missing. It suddenly dawned on me what he had been doing. Andre was wearing the new trainers to please me and stop me from nagging, but after getting out of the car in the morning, swapping them over because he preferred to wear the more comfortable ones. But this morning, I had been a little smarter than him and realised what he was up to and decided to remove the holey trainers from the bag. In this moment of realisation, Andre didn't know what to do. He kicked off the shoes on his feet and started throwing a tantrum in the back of the car, screaming that he wasn't going to go to school. As the car was already parked, I got out of the car, picked Andre up from the back seat and held him under my arm. He was small, so this was an effortless task for me, and with the shoes in the other hand, I marched with him into the school office, where I put him behind the door, dropped the shoes on the floor and walked out leaving the door to lock behind me. I would like to think that he just put the shoes on but knowing Andre, he probably just walked around all day in his socks.

I would have understood if Andre's room was full of clutter and lots of things, but it took Katy a long time to decide where to start. I'm guessing because of her job; she'd been in quite a few teenagers' bedrooms before, looking for things from either the victim or the perpetrators of crime. I had told her that Andre's bedroom looked like a prison cell. As you went in, to the right of the door was a single bed neatly made with the duvet pulled up, and the pillow fluffed. Opposite on the other side of the room was the four-square Ikea unit, and on top of it were two piles of clothes, and that was it.

"Does Andre have a laptop?" she asked me. "Or perhaps an iPad".

I shook my head in response to her questions. I was still outside of the door as I couldn't go inside. It was as if there was a force field that was repelling me from entering.

"So, what does he use to go on the Internet, play games, or speak to anybody?" she asked, looking quite confused.

"His phone", I said. "The one you have. That's all he had, just his phone", I assured her.

I guess it was strange in this day and age for people to actually own nothing. It wasn't for the want of trying. I would offer to buy Andre a new tracksuit or some trainers, but he never wanted anything. Sometimes I would force him to look online to see if there was anything that he wanted, even for a birthday or Christmas present, but he would always say there was nothing that he liked or if he was really pushed, he would pick something that was reduced in the sale. I don't really know where he got this from. Even though I wasn't a lover of expensive things, I still would like to buy myself new clothes and shoes every so often. In fact, I had loads of shoes. My husband constantly moaned about the amount of space I took up with all my different pairs of shoes, which were very rarely worn. Andre was humble; he only had what he needed, and more often than not, if Andre felt that he didn't need something anymore, he would give it away to somebody who did. This was a trait I actually loved about him, his caring nature, and his natural ability to just be free from materialistic belongings.

Katy found a carrier bag full of paperwork which she emptied out onto the bed. She flicked papers over and moved things about for a couple of minutes before deciding that there was nothing more to see. I took the opportunity to grab a few of mine and the children's belongings as we had no clothes down at my sisters, and then we headed back to Croydon. All I knew at this point regarding evidence was that there was CCTV that showed a car pulling up and people jumping out and chasing Andre. I know that he'd run. I didn't know where to, but they finally caught him. I understand that the Police were called, and paramedics were, but when they arrived at the scene, he'd lost a lot of blood. I knew they took him to the hospital, and they tried everything they could, but he didn't make it. I knew they had arrested one person in a different hospital shortly after and another one early the next day with another shortly after that. I knew all three of their identities, but a fourth was still on the run. I was waiting to hear more news about him as soon as the Police located him.

During this time, there was lots of speculation. Lots of talking, lots of hearsay about the events of what happened. There were newspaper reporters everywhere hoping to catch a piece of new information and be the first to deliver it to the public. In the past two days, there have been many newspaper articles written. We had been hunted down by the Evening Standard and local newspapers set up shop very close to the area, hoping to overhear a conversation or two. I was shocked on Friday morning when I saw a picture of myself on the front of the Croydon advertiser. Inside was a double-page spread on the information that was known at this point. Also contained within this article was word for word the spontaneous speech that I made in the local church the day after Andre was murdered. The father from the local church had come to the scene to meet my family one morning. He gave his condolences and explained that the entire estate and community were mourning for Andre. He was happy to help us with anything that we needed help with and notified us that the local church, St. Francis, would be left open during the day so that members of the community could wander in if they wanted to and light a candle or say a prayer.

We decided to visit the church and sent out a WhatsApp to let family and friends know that we would be there later in the day. I wanted to light a candle, and I needed to say a prayer. Later, as I stood at the front of the church deep in thought, I prayed to the Lord to help bring the charges to those responsible quickly, and whilst I stood there, I also spoke to Andre. I begged him to show me a sign or tell me any information I needed to know so that I could pass that on. After standing still staring up at the alter for about five to ten minutes, I turned around and was amazed that the church was packed to the brim of people from the community. As I sat in the pew trying to deal with the overwhelming feeling filling me up from the inside, I felt compelled to speak to all who had congregated.

So, this Friday morning, everything I had said in the church was written word for word. The message I was giving was mainly for the young people, for them to go in peace and not look for retaliation for what had been done so horrifically to Andre. For them to witness and understand the devastation, such crimes leave on families. I asked for the truth to be revealed and for justice to be done. I told the congregation that I didn't know how I would continue to go on without him and that it was only because of the two boys that I had stood there by my side that I knew I needed to keep living and be strong.

That evening, I was notified that the final suspect had been arrested and that the others had been charged with murder. This news hit all the major news channels as the identities of those responsible were revealed. Even though this felt like the end of the first hurdle, I knew that there were many more hurdles that I would have to overcome. For the first time in my life, I was unsettled, petrified and out of control of what was still to come. I had to dig deep, for I had work to do, and I knew that no amount of crying and falling apart would help me. It was time for me to stand up and take back some control, and it had to start the next day. This would mark the start of a very long journey, and I had so much happening.

Friday morning, after reading the Croydon Advertisers account of the previous few days, I decided that it was time to get dressed and face the day the best way I could. This day was going to be tough. Although I knew one hundred per cent that Andre was murdered that night, I still had to formally identify his body. Andre's body was being held at The Croydon Mortuary, and we agreed to meet Katy there at 11am. My Mum, sisters and Mandy were going to come to the mortuary with me to see Andre; I wasn't sure how to feel. Up until now, everything seemed so surreal. I had dropped off my healthy nineteen-year-old son, who was smiling and happy, and minutes later returned back to the same place where he was now being taken to the hospital and, within hours, being told that he was dead. Even though I had been present every step of the way, I had not witnessed any of it with my own eyes. I knew he was gone because why would anyone be so cruel to tell me that if it was untrue? But I needed to see him so that I could settle my own mind.

When we arrived, Katy briefed us on the process. Andre would be viewed from a distance. I wouldn't be able to touch him or kiss him. I needed to go in alone to have a private moment with my son, so leaving everyone outside the room, I opened the door and stepped in. The room was small. There was a wooden framed window which held a viewing glass. To each side were heavy red velvet curtains that could be drawn from the inside. Andre was laying on his back on the other side of the glass with a pillow under his head and a white sheet pulled up and tucked neatly under his neck. As I looked at him, I placed my two hands on the glass separating us. He looked so peaceful, the same way he looked when he was sleeping on my sofa wrapped in his favourite blanket. Immediately I felt pain in my chest, forehead, and the back of my eyes as I tried hard to fight back the tears that were bubbling like a volcano in my eyes.

"Andre, it's mum", I whispered. "Get up, baby".

Was our bond enough to wake him from what appeared to be a deep sleep? I focussed on his eyes, hoping to see them flickering, then all that they were telling me would be a lie, but there were none. I started to cry. Seeing Andre laying there, not moving, breathing, or responding to my voice, hurt so much. I leaned onto the glass, putting my face close against it. As I continued to sob deep inside my chest, the glass began to fog up and I frantically wiped the mist away so I could keep him in my view. I just wanted to touch him. I wanted to kiss him and tell him I was sorry for not being able to protect him from this. I needed to hold my baby in my arms and couldn't understand why they wouldn't let me. I let out an almighty scream inside, I had never felt pain like this before.

After a while, my family joined me inside the viewing gallery. We all stood there crying silently to ourselves. How could we comfort each other when we were all breaking inside? None of us wanted to leave, but after about an hour, we were told it was time for us to vacate as Andre shouldn't be left out for long. I didn't understand what that meant at the time, but it would become much more apparent later.

CHAPTER TEN
PICKING UP THE PIECES

Four were arrested within days, and four were subsequently charged with murder. The intimidation and fear that I felt during that short period of time, which felt like forever, had started to come to an end. The sleepless nights where I lay awake recalling all the images of Andre being stabbed and waking up in hot sweats not knowing where I was started to decrease. Listening to every bang or footprint as people passed by stopped sending me into a panicked state where my heart rate would raise through the ceiling and my entire body would be left trembling. I now needed to focus on my boys and give them back a level of stability so that they could feel settled and safe for the first time in a long time. Our entire lives were different. Nothing seemed familiar, and although there was no immediate risk to any of our lives, we continued to live in a hyper vigilant way, and it was controlling everything that we did daily.

Croydon Council agreed for us to move from the house in Kent to a property that they had in Streatham Common. Mandy and I went to view the flat that they had vacant as part of their emergency accommodation scheme with the plan to move over the next few days. We sat outside Topps Tiles in a red route waiting for the landlord to arrive. There were commercial sized bins outside the property entrance that were overflowing with rubbish. Dirty underwear strewed across the ground and millions of flies feeding off the leftovers that were not hygienically disposed of. I wanted to cry. This is what I would have to walk past every time I came in and out of the flat. Maybe inside was better? The entrance hall downstairs was full of graffiti and rubbish bins. There was a smell of food and urination in the stairwell as we made our way to the top of the building. Artificial lighting was non-existent, and the only time light came into view was when we reached the balcony with its broken metal poles that a whole child could fit through. The inside wasn't as bad. A few broken tiles and mattresses and bed bases that looked as if they should have been thrown out alongside the other piles of rubbish downstairs. I left the debating for Mandy, who was equally as shocked by the conditions of the property as I was. I needed to take it. I was in no position at the moment to refuse any help that was offered. I couldn't stay in Kent; my baby was laying in Croydon Mortuary, and I needed to be closer to my family and friends for support. I accepted the property and the following day a group of us travelled to Kent to pack the remainder of our belongings. Andre's friend had borrowed us his van so that we could move everything in one go. Lorraine's husband Ray drove the van for me and the rest of us travelled down in our cars. A quick in and out. That's all I wanted to do. As everyone helped to pack the kitchen, bathroom and living room up into boxes and bags, I made my way to Andre's room. Every part of my inner being was pulled apart as I ran my hands over his clothing and sniffed Andre's jumpers and pillows. I could smell him, and I never wanted to lose that smell, so I packed his belongings into bags and placed them into my car. This was all that I had left of my son's life, and it hurt so bad.

Everyone volunteered their help that day. I was extremely grateful as well as being exhausted. Exhausted from not just the physical aspects of moving but the emotional turmoil that it caused throughout. I was now back in Croydon, on the outskirts but closer to everything that I needed right now. The boys would be able to return to their schools in September if the felt ready and I would be able to start making any necessary plans knowing that I didn't need to drive so far away.

One evening Amari and I went to the shop to get snacks to take home. Normally once we were inside, we were in, with the doors locked and the windows secured. We were walking back to the car parked outside of the shop, and as I climbed into the driver's seat, ready to head home, I noticed that Amari's body language had changed dramatically. Amari was staring through the car's window screen, still and silent. It scared me because I, being hyper vigilant, hadn't picked up on anything that could be deemed as remotely risky.

"What's wrong?" I asked him as he remained frozen in his seat fixated and staring through the window screen.

Unexpectedly, Amari jumped out of the seat he was sitting on and flew over the space between the chairs where we sat onto my lap.

Something had frightened him. He held onto me for dear life, and it felt as though if he could have climbed inside my body for safety, he would have. I held him close to me as I took to looking out of the window too. I could feel his little heart beating against mine and he was wriggling as if to get further away from the passenger side of the car. Walking towards the car was a young man who very much resembled one of those charged with Andre's murder. It startled me as my emotional brain started to take over and I instinctively banged on the button to lock all the car doors. I pulled my rational brain back, telling myself that it wasn't possible for it to be him, and my fear started to disappear. He was the same height and had the same complexion but more than that, he had the same hairstyle, messy twists. I could see why Amari would have been afraid.

"It's not him", I tried to reassure him as the boy moved past the car.

After a few minutes, Amari relaxed and sat back in his seat. I had a seriously affected eight-year-old, and for me, this was one of the first signs of trauma and fear that I had seen aside from his sleepless nights and the tantrums. How was I going to help Amari ever feel safe again? When we arrived back home, we followed a routine of using our phone torches to navigate the dark stairwells up to our front door. One night there was a group of young men in the stairs smoking cannabis. Both boys were trembling and holding onto my clothes as we navigated our way past the unfamiliar people, dodging the cables that were hanging from the ceiling and climbing over the rubbish on the corner of each landing. I couldn't believe that I was living like this, my ability to make choices had been taken away from me. Not only with housing but with my son.

It was clear that Streatham common was not the place for us, it was too busy, and there were too many things happening around that we had to be aware of. I still find it difficult to comprehend the thought process of the staff at Croydon Council and how they could not show a greater level of empathy for a family that had just had their entire world turned upside down. One particular morning that stands out in my mind was early in September, once the children had returned back to school. I had the most horrendous night and hadn't slept. The noises of other residents moving around in their flats, the slamming of doors, Police and Ambulance sirens which triggered every nerve in my body and the rowdy passer-buyers who would scream, swear, and fight as they made their way home from late-night drinking was taking its toll on me. After dropping the boys to school, I drove back home, thinking I could put my head down for a few hours just to try and catch up on some much-needed sleep. The flat which sat above a Tile store, although high up, was very overlooked. There were no net or heavy curtains in the flat, so on this particular day, the sun was beaming in through the windows, and the workman working on the scaffolding around the building opposite were peering in through the windows like meerkats.

I lay on the stiff white tub leather sofa, which had really high arms, so it was almost impossible to get comfortable on and I started to cry. I couldn't stop crying. I didn't know how my life had got to this. I was missing Andre so badly, and the place that I was living and the lack of parenting that I was able to give to the boys were contributing to the spiralling amount of depression that I was feeling. It had taken me almost an hour to park the car and come upstairs, and during this time, I had made a call to Croydon Council to discuss other options for housing. It was a desperate plea for help when I was feeling at my lowest. After being connected to a housing advisor and giving my name, and briefly explaining my issues with the flat that I was currently living in, the housing advisor responded in a way that shattered me inside.

"Well, you should be grateful that you have two other children," she said.

I hung the phone up, almost immediately without responding. This was one of the most insensitive comments that I had heard in a long time. Of course, I was grateful for all my children, but that wasn't the issue. I had one missing. One that had been murdered on the streets of Croydon, and for the first time in years, I needed some help. Help to feel safe! Help to feel settled! Help to be able to come home to a place that I could make feel a little bit like home again, surrounded by some of our belongings that would hopefully give us a sense of normality back. Since living in Streatham, we had already had a break-in. A previous tenant thought that it would be acceptable to break open the kitchen window with a crowbar, climb in to open the front door and then proceed to remove the furniture that I had just finished arranging before the boys came home. The previous tenant took the sofa out, which resulted in me having to purchase a second-hand sofa for us to sit on. The one that I was currently laying on bawling my eyes out. They also proceeded to enter the main bedroom and take the wardrobe that was situated inside the room. I was devastated when I came home, not just by the fact that someone had broken into our makeshift home and stolen the furniture but also that they had taken Andre's clothes that I had neatly folded and packed into the bottom of the wardrobe and threw them across the floor. They would not have known that they were disrespecting the belongings of my recently deceased son, but their actions in their entirety were inappropriate and had caused my family great distress. Apart from repairing the window, the private landlord had no urgency to put this issue right, including replacing the missing items of furniture or placing a mortice lock on the door to make us feel extra secure when at home. I knew that I couldn't stay here, and this is when I decided that I would email the council daily until they considered me for alternative emergency accommodation.

It actually didn't take long. Within days the council contacted me to let me know that they only had one private emergency accommodation available and that if I didn't take the property, they would not be able to offer me anything else. Andre appeared in every newspaper for months, and this made the case quite high profile. I think that this sometimes helped as people especially those who lived within the Croydon borough, felt obliged through sympathy to help my family and me. I agreed to the property and had been instructed to move the same evening. The new property was a three-bedroom house in Forestdale. Geographically the estate, although lovely was situated almost opposite the Monks Hill Estate, where Andre was murdered almost four weeks earlier. I had severely mixed feelings about being back in this neighbourhood. Although it felt familiar, every time I did that drive home, it felt like the same drive I took on the evening in August when I received that panicked phone call to inform me that Andre had been stabbed. Being back in the neighbourhood also meant that Ashley was able to reach out quite easily and meet up with his former friends. I still had burning questions about why Andre was left alone outside the Spar waiting for his friends and why they never turned up but why instead, those four boys turned up brandishing weapons to take my son's life away.

The truth is I didn't trust anyone! I didn't want anyone to know where we lived, and I didn't even want the boys to be seen out and about alone.

I had a fourteen-year-old who was struggling to deal with his emotions and how he was feeling regarding his brother's death, and he desperately wanted to try to get some normality back in his life and be around other young people that he was able to speak to, especially because they knew his brother and were actually there the night that he was chased through the streets and stabbed. I, however wanted to wrap them both up in cotton wool and protect them from the world so that no one could ever cause them any harm. Ashley and I found ourselves in arguments on most days. I just couldn't understand why he would think it was ok to go to the Monks Hill estate, to the youth club or just to a friend's house. I didn't even want to drive in the neighbourhood, let alone mix with anyone, and he didn't want my overbearing protection. Some days I had the strength to stand my ground, and others, I was just too weak to fight with him. I was struggling badly to get myself together and found that the only thing that gave me any comfort or the ability to sleep was alcohol. And I had no preference. It could have been Brandy or Rum. It didn't matter. I wanted it so I drank it. After a few weeks, the children noticed that I had been drinking a lot. It wasn't intentional, but people seemed to bring a bunch of flowers and a bottle of drink to my house, and when they did this, I drank it. I would go to bed to sleep and take a hot coffee upstairs with me. What I thought the children didn't know was that it was laced with rum. After a mug of coffee topped with a large shot of rum, I would be able to sleep quite peacefully until my dreams or, better described, nightmares, got the better of me, and I would wake up in a dark room sweating profusely. I had a large box of anti-depressants and various sleeping pills, but instead of taking these, I decided that my homemade alcoholic cocktails would work just fine. I've never been a fan of taking medication unless it was really necessary. Against the advice of the doctor and my own mother, who was taking her own prescribed medication to help her to cope with the loss of her first-born grandson, I just couldn't bring myself to do it. I could drink at night to help me sleep and then leave it alone all day.

I wasn't really a drinker prior to this. I was always the nominated driver when my friends and I went out at the weekend. I would have one or maybe two drinks, stop, and still have a great night out, getting everyone home safely. I think it's because I am so independent and always have been. I liked to be in control of my actions at all times. If I drank and didn't drive, I would have to rely on someone else to drop me home at a time that suited them and most of the time with my friends, that would be when the birds were chirping. These nights out are what often caused the most issues with my husband. He was twelve years older than me and hadn't become a father for the first time until he was in his thirties. He had already had the wild nights out with his friends, gained all of those life experiences before his first child was born and gained the parenting responsibility, that I had for years before. I used to desperately try to explain to him that I had been a teenage mum and had missed out on the nightlife as a teenager and in my early twenties. After having my third son at twenty-nine, I wanted to let my hair down a bit and have some of the girly nights out that I had missed out on in my younger years. He didn't understand this or even want to compromise, and this caused so many nights of arguing, hiding keys, letting down tyres and sometimes even physical altercations. On reflection, I feel that if we could have come to a compromise back then, we would have still been together now.

One afternoon when my sister came over, I had written a stupid statement on Facebook about having enough and not wanting to do it anymore, I put myself to bed and switched off my phone. This caused a massive pandemonium as everyone presumed it was a suicide note when really, I was talking about the amount of alcohol I was drinking. She came into the bedroom that I had blacked out the windows of and was sleeping and sobbing simultaneously to check if I was alright. Lorraine, my eldest sister, asked the boys if I was drinking, and this is when the youngest told her.

"Mum has a bottle of rum behind the bed, but she doesn't think that we know that it is there."

This was my wake-up call. What was I doing to my babies? They should not know that I was drinking the amount I was, I felt disgusted with myself. The boys were cleaning up the kitchen, and I was watching them through the living room window putting the recycling out. The number of empty bottles they were dropping into the recycling bin made me feel appalled. This was not the person that I wanted to be, and this was definitely going to affect the boys if I didn't stop. Although I didn't stop drinking entirely, I did cut down. I never consumed anything unless they were asleep in bed, and I stopped hiding bottles of alcohol around the house. I needed to pull myself together, but really all I wanted to do was escape.

As the days rolled past, there were several days when I just couldn't cope with the overwhelming level of emotion that I was feeling. I was exhausted and clearly going through all the different stages of grief, shock, denial, anger, guilt, bargaining, depression, and acceptance. I was in shock, and that stayed the same every day. I found myself talking to myself, telling myself that Andre was gone and then questioning whether that information was really true or not. I used to walk through all the steps in my mind leading up to receiving the terrible news in the hospital, reliving every conversation to work out if a huge mistake had been made. I would catch Amari staring at me, and when I asked him what was wrong, he would ask who I was speaking to. I still do this now, especially if I am deep in thought.

I was so angry. I was mad at Andre, which hurt so much because I could no longer have those long conversations with him where we could reason and work through the things that had gone wrong in his life. He would always come home, lay on the bed with me, and tell me the ins and outs of his day. Good, bad, or ugly, he was always honest, and that is how we built the bond that we had. I wanted to ask him why he didn't listen to me. Why did he not trust my judgement, my gut instinct? Why, when he had that feeling that something was wrong, he didn't go into someone's house or leave immediately and call me. He always called me, and I was angry that this time had been different.

I found myself bargaining. Often late at night, after a few drinks when the children were asleep and the house was in silence, I would ask God to please let me have him back. I would promise to do a barrage of different things better or just swap him with me so that he could live the life he was entitled to, and I could go and be in peace. I knew that losing a parent was hard for children. I had learned this by watching Samantha's two children after she passed away, but I was sure that the pain I was feeling as a parent for losing my first-born son had to be more complex. It was not the natural order, and it felt so wrong, so any bargaining that I could do, I did it.

I was definitely depressed, but I was nowhere near ready to even consider acceptance. Throughout the days and weeks to come, I continued in this cycle of stages of grief. I had many down days where I could have quite easily curled up in a ball and died myself, but I thought about the boys and how two sudden deaths would affect them, and I knew this would never be an option. They both appeared to be coping. Ashley was definitely more vocal about how he was feeling, but the one that worried me the most was Amari. How was an eight-year-old supposed to process everything that was going on? He started off by having three to four tantrums a day. Screaming, kicking his feet, and absolutely trashing everything in his way. The strange thing for me was that there were no tears at all. The noise was coming out of his mouth, and the actions that he was displaying were definitely that of anger, but there were no tears. We slept in the same bed with the lights on every night. Amari and I, that is. Ashley, as much as we begged him to join us with all the single beds pushed together, he declined and went to bed alone with the lights off and the door shut. I don't know how he did it, but he just did.

The nights became better once Lilie started to stay over. Lilie was friends with Andre, they had gone to the same secondary school. Andre was most definitely an agony aunt, and he had several young ladies who he spent the nights talking through their problems with. I know that they were struggling. During their time of grief, the person that they needed to talk to was sadly the one missing. Lilie lived within walking distance to where we were now, and her presence not only helped me as she was able to entertain Amari, cook, help me with the cleaning up and just generally be someone else in the house, but I think that her being with us helped her too. She was able to share her memories with us, and I believe that she gained some peace of mind knowing that she was supporting Andre's mum and siblings as he would have probably wanted.

Some days I just needed my mum. I really tried hard not to let my mum know what was happening in terms of the investigation and the evidence that was coming out about the case and what had happened to Andre because I really didn't want to put any more weight on her than she was already carrying. Mums always want to be there for their children, and she really was trying, but the truth was that I was a much stronger person than my mum. I felt like I needed to help support her and my sisters, and as long as I could see that they were holding up that gave me one less thing that I needed to worry about. I had gone to my mum's house because I was having a hard day. A day where I just couldn't get myself to settle emotionally. It had been so long since I had seen Andre. I had never been separated from him before, and as the days passed, the feeling of longing to see him were become more intense.

I could sleep at my mum's house knowing that she would take care of everything. She would keep herself busy by cooking for the family and entertaining her grandsons. I couldn't get the feeling of missing Andre out of my system. The last time I had seen him was the day that I had to go and identify his body and not being able to touch him left me feeling an agonising pain and an emptiness in the pit of my stomach. I decided to call the Mortuary and enquire whether I could go again to see him. Unlike an average death of someone of old age or illness, within days, you would be able to visit the funeral home to view the body, but Andre was still being kept inside the Mortuary, and I didn't like the feeling it was giving me. I had watched dramas on the television where they slide the bodies in and out of the wall, and that is all I could visualise every time I thought about my baby.

I called the number I was given and explained who I was and that I wanted to come back and see my son. The lady on the other end of the phone referred me to someone else in the Mortuary, and the news she gave me was not what I wanted to hear.

"Sorry!", she said. "We won't be able to authorise for you to see Andre because his body has been out too many times for the autopsies that have needed to take place, and if he continues to be removed, his body will deteriorate too quickly."

I was absolutely horrified. What did they mean by autopsies? More than one? How could somebody that I made, carried, birthed and raised now be the property of the mortuary and me, his mother, cannot even see him when I want to. I hung up the phone and sobbed into my mum's pillow until I fell asleep.

Later that evening I called Katy. There were so many questions that I needed answering and she was the only person that I knew that could possibly give me them. Katy explained that each defendant had the right to autopsy to use in their defence. Hearing this made me feel physically sick. What a disgusting rule which violated any rights that myself of Andre, even in death, had. I spent the evening looking up the process of autopsies and it devastated me.

CHAPTER ELEVEN
PLANNING THE FUNERAL

It was now six weeks since Andre had been murdered, and I was becoming extremely frustrated with the lack of information that was coming forward about when we could have his body back. The funeral would be an essential part of the grieving process for our family and holding the funeral would mean that we could lay him to rest and get some closure on this part, at least.

I contacted our family liaison officer, Katy, to find out how long this would take. Surly after six weeks, they had everything they needed to create a strong enough case and make the convictions stand up in court for those responsible for taking my beautiful boys' life away. She tried hard to reassure me that the funeral would be able to take place in the next two weeks and advised me to start making the arrangements. I called a family meeting. I needed the family's input to gauge what they thought would be the best things to do. The one thing that I was sure of was that it was going to be in true Andre style. Andre was a simple appreciative person, and he definitely wasn't a show-off whatsoever. Hence, although I wanted his final send-off to be the best possible, I also knew that it needed to reflect him and the life he had lived for the short time that he was here.

Everyone gathered at my house, crammed onto the makeshift furniture of my temporary accommodation. This is never something you expect to be doing for your child, and the atmosphere in the room reflected this. Although everyone that was there knew that this was a meaningful conversation that needed to be had, nobody really wanted to have it. We talked through the plans for the day, the day that even though I wished would hurry up and come, I actually didn't want to have to do. One thing I knew about Andre was that he absolutely loved Monks Hill. Why would he not? He grew up there, and it's where he had some of his fondest memories. As painful as it felt to include this place where he was finally hunted down and stabbed to death, it needed to be done, and I know that this would have been his wish if he was sat here with us making these plans. There was the local church, St Francis, at the top of the estate; although I don't think Andre had even ever been in the church, I am sure that he attended local activities that the church held in the summer holidays when he was younger. This was also the place where my sister Hayley ran her slimming business. She struggled like me to even go to the estate to keep her classes running. This impacted her so severely, and she finally decided that the continuous drive through the estate was too painful for her, so she moved the group to a different venue. The number of changes everyone affected by Andre's murder had to make to deal with the pain and loss they were feeling was immense. If only the perpetrators had thought about the impact on Andre's family and friends, they wouldn't have done it. The need to prove a point and save face to the extremes that they took up a knife intending to take his life without any thoughts about the consequences of their actions baffled me.

It was agreed that I would speak to the father at the church so that the funeral service could be held on the estate with the local community attending if they so wished. The funeral director I had already instructed to liaise with the mortuary was Rowland Brothers, situated on Whitehorse Road. This was the obvious choice for me as not only was it the road that I had spent my childhood growing up on, but it was also the funeral director responsible for most of the family funerals I had been to. A family friend also worked for them, and it comforted me that she would look after Andre and do the best for him when he finally arrived.

Purple & Blue would be the themed colours as they were Andre's favourite. Andre went to secondary school at Oasis Shirley Park, the school that I was still working at when he was murdered, and the school's colour was Purple. When Andre was in Year nine, he made me buy him a purple puffer jacket which he wore with pride. He justified being able to wear it because it was in the school's colours, and he absolutely loved it. Every time there was an issue at the school and staff needed to watch the CCTV to ascertain what had happened, there would be Andre, who was the smallest in height and build in his year group, standing out like a sore thumb because of the purple jacket. When I started working there, the Deputy Heads would turn up at my classroom with the jacket in their hands and ask me to keep it for the remainder of the day. Even though it very often had him caught out or placed at the scene of whatever was happening that day, it also helped to eliminate him from many incidents. If the staff couldn't see the jacket, then as far as they were concerned, Andre wasn't there or involved. One day the fire alarm was set off in the school, which resulted in over one thousand students and staff having to exit the building in a timely manner to line up in the designated areas outside. The Headteacher at the time was the most fantastic leader and head any school could have asked for. He was a man huge in stature but spoke like a gentle giant. He shook every young person's hand in the morning as they walked to school and greeted them with a smile and a good morning.

"Sir", I said as I approached him in the corridor. "I noticed you had Andre in your office. Did he set off the alarm?" I asked, slightly embarrassed.

"No", he replied. "It wasn't Andre."

I was curious, had the CCTV been checked yet or was Andre just not in the purple jacket at the time, so unrecognisable?

"Are you sure?" I enquired further

The Headteacher looked at me with an expression on his face to appease me from the anguish I was feeling.

"Mum", he said. "I asked Andre if it was him, and he said no. That's good enough for me! One thing I can say about your son is that If I ask him, he always tells me the truth even if it means he will get into trouble. If he did, he will always admit it and take the consequences that are to follow. I respect that about him"

This was one hundred per cent accurate. I knew that Andre was like this. No matter what he did, he was honest. I respected him for that as I always knew where I stood with him; nothing was a surprise, ever!

Andre liked blue clothes, and they suited him. The day he was murdered, he wore a blue north face tee shirt that he had not long brought himself. After the purple jacket faze, he moved onto a blue puffer jacket. It did something to his eyes. Many of the photos circulated of Andre after he died saw him wearing blue tee shirts, jumpers, coats, and hats. Blue needed to be included in his final arrangements. So many people offered to help, and it was so appreciated. My old school friends and people I hadn't even spoken to in years were reaching out to me left, right and centre. Heidi, who trained as a florist, sent me a message on Facebook offering her support with the flower arrangements for the funeral. Heidi also lived on Monks Hill, and her daughter had been a friend of Andre, unbeknown to me. Andre knew everyone. When I say that the entire community was affected by his death, I precisely mean just that. The outpouring that there was for support to plan or contribute was terrific. I had never felt this amount of support in my life. It was, at times, very overwhelming. I would lay in bed at night reading all the messenger messages I was receiving, and comments left on online newspaper articles, and it would always reduce me to tears. I just prayed that Andre knew how loved he really was. I knew it was all because of him. Andre was a unique type of boy; I knew this, but it could have been perceived as a bias coming from me, his mother, but it was evident at this time that this was the same feeling that everyone else that knew him had, so it definitely could not have just been a bias on my part.

After approaching the Father at St Francis Church, he advised us that although he would have been honoured to hold the service at the church on the estate, he didn't feel that it was going to be the right place because it only held a small number of people inside. As a pillar of the community, I think that he knew that it would be a well-attended funeral and that the space he had just wouldn't be able to accommodate all those that wished to pay their respects. We played around with many different ideas, including using a hall space inside the church and the outside area to project the service via video link. Still, eventually, we agreed to visit another church in Selsdon just a short way away at the bottom of the main high street that would hold up to at least five hundred people.

On the day we visited the church, I had the most overwhelming feeling take over my entire body. As I walked into the church through the main entrance, a beam of light shone through the stained-glass windows in the ceiling. I instantly burst out crying, knowing this was the right place. When I think about it now, I believe that Andre was guiding me throughout the entire process. As stated before, in the early evening, when I dropped Andre off, the beam of sunlight that was shining on him gave me a feeling of warmth, and it is an image that I still cannot get out of my mind. It was as if the Lord was shining down on him a ray from heaven, and this is the same feeling I felt when I walked into the church that day. A church hall was next to the church, and we booked both for the funeral on the 19th of October 2016.

With the church and hall booked, we went back to the funeral directors to make the arrangements for once Andre's body was received. It is the most awful thing you ever have to do to sit around a table looking through a catalogue of coffins you might wish to purchase for your son to be placed in. Although Andre was legally classed as an adult at nineteen, he was still a child; my baby and I knew that the coffin he needed to be in was a white one. Not only was it a symbol of innocence, but a child. I also thought that it was what he would have wanted, simplicity! Mandy offered to pay for the coffin, which was around six hundred pounds. This was a huge relief because, at this point, I had absolutely no idea how I would pay for the funeral. Andre's sister had set up a go-fund-me account to raise money to support us with the funeral costs. At the time, I was annoyed that this had happened because I hadn't been asked. To be honest, I felt embarrassed to ask for financial support; now, I had become very appreciative and overwhelmed by the level of support that the members of my community were showing. It didn't matter whether they knew Andre, our family, or empathised with our current situation; this was a journey they wouldn't wish on their worst enemies.

The most challenging part of planning a funeral for me was the day I had to go to the cemetery to select a plot for my son's final resting place. I felt that this was something that I needed to do with Andre's Father, so we arranged an appointment and made our way there. I left home in the morning to drop the boys off at school and stopped at the Shell Petrol Station on Addington Road to fill up my car. After dropping both boys to school, I drove around Davidson Road to make my way to the cemetery. The car was jolting, and I was finding it extremely difficult to pick up speed. As I struggled to drive the car even in first gear, it finally gave up on the main road, and I was stranded. I called Andre's Dad to let him know what had happened, and he drove around to pick me up.

My relationship with Andre's Dad had always been an amicable one. When Andre was nine months old, he decided to emigrate to America to live where his mother and sisters had all resided for several years. I was only seventeen when I had Andre, and although it was not a planned pregnancy, I wanted him so much. His Dad was not as convinced that it was the right thing to do then, but as we didn't have a relationship regarded as being 'serious', he respected my wishes. I'm not going to lie and pretend that he stepped up to the plate or deserved a father of the year award because he didn't. He had been, at times, an absent father to Andre. It was a shame because they were so similar, and you could see his personality developing more in Andre as he grew up. He did, however, always keep in touch. He would call and speak to his son. He would send trainers and clothes for Andre at every opportunity. If he hadn't invited another woman to visit him in America, who then went on to have a child for him, Andre's younger sister, I probably would have made more of an effort to travel out there to be with him.

Even though it was a difficult situation in the early days of having Andre, as soon as he returned from America after fifteen years, he insisted on coming to meet up with Andre and building a relationship with him. Regardless of the situation, he loved his son and having him murdered was taking its toll on him. He thought I couldn't see him struggling, but I could. He was a dithering mess. He couldn't get his words together, and he could not express how he was feeling. He had been at the hospital the night Andre had died because I made sure that I had called him along with my husband, Andre's stepdad. His return to England caused issues in my marriage because my husband didn't feel I should have allowed him to come back into Andre's life. I let it for one simple reason – he was his biological father, and Andre was at an age where he could decide whether he wanted to have a father-son relationship with his dad or not. I would never stop my children from seeing their fathers, they were not physically abusive or harmful, so I had always tried to keep the channels of communication open to them.

We arrived at the cemetery after abandoning my car, and the cemetery staff took us on a tour of the grounds and then finally to the area they were currently using for new burials. I watched as the lady leading us pointed to different plots that were available.

"This one.......... and this one here, you can have this one," she said as we continued to climb over a few more graves and then said, "This one's free."

How was I supposed to choose one over another? After all, it was just a hole in the ground that would be dug six feet deep and then my son would be put inside. What makes it an appropriate place to select? What criteria do parents use to pick a plot for their children? Eventually, we reached a quieter part of the cemetery just off a small pathway, and we were shown a plot that was not overcrowded and only had one grave in front of it and nothing to one of the sides but grass and a neatly trimmed bush.

"This one is available", the cemetery worker explained.

Just as she was about to state that it was a reclaimed grave – meaning that someone had previously been buried in the same plot and it had been cleared out ready for a new burial, I stopped her in her tracks. There was no way that Andre's Dad would agree to put Andre in a reclaimed grave, and if he had heard her state that, then we would have had to carry on looking. The truth is that the cemetery was overcrowded and the area we were in was all reclaimed. As I would probably be the one to spend the most amount of time at the cemetery, I needed to make sure that it was somewhere that I felt comfortable standing. As I looked around, I noticed the grave of David Darko, who had been murdered in a local park in January of the same year. Andre had gone to school with David's brother and knowing that he was just there gave me some comfort.

"We will take this one," I said.

Someone had to decide, and to be honest, as long as it felt okay for me, it didn't really matter what others thought. Death and funerals had been a topic of conversation in my house long before Andre was murdered. Some of Andre's friends were reckless, and I often told them off when they came over. I would lecture them about drinking, smoking, getting into fights or just being out late at night without a purpose. When all this started with Andre and his friends, after the first shooting, I had them all in the living room one day, and I was reading them the riot act like any worried mother would.

"Listen", I said. I can't afford to bury anyone, so stay out of trouble.

As I stood there in the cemetery, I recalled the words that Andre had said to me that day.

"Don't worry about that, mum; if anything happens to me, just dig a hole on Monks and put me in it".

Thinking back to this conversation, which he said so flippantly at the time, I felt sure about my decisions. Andre didn't expect to die. Not for one moment, when he made that comment, nor did he think it was something I would be organising in the next few weeks. The family had conversations about whether to bury or cremate Andre. I was very much for burials because I felt I needed somewhere to go, and his brothers would benefit from knowing that his body was laid to rest somewhere they could visit when they wanted to. When the time had come to explain my decision to my family, it was solely based on this conversation I had with my son weeks earlier. Had he said, "build a bonfire and throw me on it, " maybe I would have considered a cremation.

I was overwhelmed; I had so many things I needed to sort out. Having the church, church hall and now the plot arranged meant I could turn to the finer details to make sure that my son's send-off was the best that I could possibly make it. Financially, I was not in a good place, but my family and friends were pulling all the strings they could to ensure that the financial burden didn't rest on me; for that, I will always be grateful. I wrote a list of things I needed to organise and delegated different parts of Andre's final journey to other people. I tried hard to include everyone in this because I didn't know if I had the strength, I needed at the time to plan and carry out this day, but I also wanted them to be involved, including my fourteen-year-old son.

Ashley's role was to organise printed tee shirts for everyone to wear. Mandy was managing the catering. My sisters were sourcing table decorations for the wake, and I handled everything else. My friend had volunteered to make the flowers for the funeral and set a date with me to purchase all we needed. We drove to the wholesalers, and I watched her professionally and strategically choose all the flowers. She picked the ribbon and accessories needed to create the spray for the top of the coffin and the words SON, BRO and ANDRE as wreaths that I wanted for the sides of the hearse. I thought this was going to be a lot of work for her, and I didn't want it to seem like I was taking liberties, so I offered to help her. I had never attempted flower arranging before; at home, when I even put flowers into a vase, I found it challenging to place them in a beautiful way. My friend felt it might help me to be involved in the process, and she was right. I found it so therapeutic. Sitting at her dining room table adding ribbon to the edges of the letters, most importantly, just talking. She probably doesn't know how much she helped me during this time. It was a very personal thing that she was doing, especially as she knew my son, and we had both known each other since secondary school. I was grateful for the time she gave and allowed me to help make the beautiful wreaths that would join Andre in the hearse on his final journey.

I couldn't stop. I became a complete control freak. I had to control everything about the day from start to finish. I was running on adrenaline, and I couldn't stop it. Whenever I thought that I had covered everything, I thought of something else I could do to make the day memorable for him. Andre had written and recorded a couple of music tracks. I wasn't very impressed by the track's lyrical content, but I did know that he had musical talent. From the day after Andre's passing, the young people had repeatedly played his track. I had heard it so many times I knew all the lyrics myself. Hearing his voice would instantly make me well up, and the tears would flow. What I would give to listen to that voice one more time. I thought about how I could use his voice for his funeral. I had an idea to mix Andre's track with another track for the entry to the church. I played the picture over and over in my head so many times before I finally decided that I would do it. I spoke to a close friend of mine who was a DJ. If anyone could mix music together, he could, so one evening, we met up and went through different tracks until we came to

Mariah Carey's One Sweet Day. He worked to take Andre's voice and create a way where he started first and then blended the chosen song with his. We played around with it for hours. I cried uncontrollably, and he held me in his arms to comfort me. Eventually, the track was completed. I had such good people around me. Everyone was doing everything that they could to support me. The same friend organised for Doves to be released at the funeral and offered to play music at the wake. These were all areas that I hadn't even thought of prior, and again I was so grateful for the support I was getting.

CHAPTER TWELVE
ANDRE'S FINAL FAREWELL

There was one final thing I needed to do, and the phone call I had been waiting for from the funeral home came just a few days before the funeral. I had already purchased Andre a new tracksuit and sliders to be buried in, and my mum had brought him an angel pendant to wear around his neck. These had all been dropped off days earlier, along with the beanie hat I wanted him to wear. Andre never went out in the cold without his hat on his head, and it was October after all and getting very chilly. I had a house full of family members when I received the call to say that Andre was dressed and being moved into the chapel of rest. The only person I told was Mandy as I didn't want the children to come with me when I visited him. I had a yearning feeling in my stomach for the past eight weeks. It was like a pulling sensation that I guess only mothers feel when they are missing their children. Without saying a word, I jumped in the car and headed to the funeral home to meet Mandy. I was ready to see my son. It had been such a long time, and even though I had been warned that it wouldn't be pleasant to witness, I didn't care. I needed to see my baby one last time before the funeral.

As I drove, the strangest thing happened to me. I could hear Andre's voice as clear as day speaking to me.

"Mum, Mum, don't go there", the voice said. It spooked me, but I knew it was him.

"Don't go there, mum!" the voice begged me.

Why was I hearing him? I shook it off and continued on my journey, where I met Mandy outside. Once inside the funeral home, we met with the director, who sat us down in the bright and airy lobby.

"Yemi, are you sure you want to see Andre?" she asked me.

I wasn't sure but I was missing him so badly and had waited for so long, that seemed like the only option I had at the time to halt the yearning that I was feeling.

"I need to warn you that his body is not in a very good condition at all, and we wouldn't recommend that you view him", she continued to tell me.

She explained that Andre's body couldn't be adequately embalmed because there were too many holes in his body from the injuries. Hearing this made me feel physically sick. I was also aware that the clothing I had brought for him had to be cut and wrapped around his fragile body. He had been wrapped in bandages like a mummy from his ankles to his neck, and this was the only way they could see to dress him. I really wish that they had told me sooner. The thought that he wasn't wearing the clothes I had chosen, and his ring was not on his finger or sliders on his feet left me with a feeling of discontent. I could have made different decisions if I had been notified. Maybe they felt it was too much information for me to deal with. I could have purchased an Arsenal duvet and pillow and had him wrapped up asleep like he would have been when at home. I would have preferred that to how he was now being presented. Despite what she had to say, I still needed to see my boy. Knowing he was there and within meters of me made me severely nervous. After a brief exchange of words with Mandy, we signed paperwork to say that we had been advised but chosen to see him anyway. Could it really be that bad? I had wanted to see Andre days ago when he was first brought to the funeral home from the mortuary, but when I enquired on the day in question, I was informed that this wouldn't be possible.

"We will have to leave Andre to defrost for the weekend. We use a liquid that we have to pour over his body to help with this process and then embalm him before a viewing can take place", I was told.

I will never be able to get the image that I built up in my mind out. I could picture Andre laying frozen like a chicken on a stainless-steel table in a sterile room. The liquid I envisaged was blue, like anti-freeze dripping from his lifeless body and dropping onto the white tiled floor. Even now, when I see frozen chickens in the supermarket, it throws me straight back to that image, which is probably half the reason why I stopped eating meat a few years later.

As we walked down the corridor towards the chapel where Andre was laid, we tried to make light of the situation. Still, I could see that the funeral director was genuinely worried, and as we stopped outside the large wooden doors that opened up into the chapel, Mandy decided that she should go in first just to check and that I should come in afterwards. My heart was banging inside my chest. I was scared about what I might see, yet I was pining for my son. I watched as Mandy entered the room. As I stood outside, I tried to catch a glimpse of him through the crack in the door opening. I could see the white coffin we had selected lined up against the wall, and my boy was inside. My heartbeat rapidly, and I tried to hold back the tears. His placement meant I could only see the top of his head covered by the beanie hat I had brought to keep his head warm. As I continued to look, I could see an ear poking up over the top of the hat and then, as I stood trying to work out where the hat finished and his face began, Mandy came bundling out of the room with haste and a look of horror on her face. As she approached me, closely followed by the funeral director, she spun me around and pushed me up the corridor away from the door.

"You're not going in there she said!" as she continued to direct me with some force back up the corridor and away from where my Andre lay.

I became confused and disorientated but most of all scared, and as we picked up the pace, I started to run. I ran up the corridor, past the reception and out the front door leaving the sound of the bell ringing in the background as I continued to run up Whitehorse Road. As I continued to run, unsure of where I was running to, I could hear Mandy calling me in the background. I stopped. The pavement was spinning, and I felt dizzy. My heart was pounding like someone was beating a big bass drum, and I was crying uncontrollably. As the cars whizzed by me, going about their daily business, I was stood on the edge of the main road, bent over, vomiting as if my life depended on it. After a short while, Mandy caught up with me, and we left.

"What happened?" I asked her.

"It didn't look like him, Yem. Andre is not there", she explained.

But that wasn't what caused her to run. Mandy heard Andre. She heard him laughing as she looked at him laying in his coffin. Just as I had listened to his voice as clear as day on the drive down. What he had said to her resembled what happened at my sister Lorraine's house about a week before he passed. He was playing us off against each other. He was jokingly swearing at me by mouthing out a rude word behind my sister's back, and when I asked her to sort her nephew out, he sat there like butter wouldn't melt in his mouth until he erupted into laughter. Mandy didn't know this at the time, but it is now a memory that I treasure. Andre was so jovial, and this is something that I could imagine him doing in life if we were being nosey. Once home, I called the funeral home and instructed them to do three things which I felt would be what Andre would want. Remove the makeup from his face. Andre's complexion had become so dark, which I now know happens after death. There is no way that he would have wanted makeup on his face either; he definitely would have had something to say about that. To pull the hat down over his ears just like he would wear it and finally put him away and not let anyone else attempt to view his body. I think Andre had made his point loud and clear; all I could do was try to honour it.

The day finally arrived. There was nothing more that I could do. All arrangements had been made, and the day needed to play out. I woke up at 5am. I probably hadn't slept at all that night. I tossed and turned, contemplating the day. I came downstairs, leaving the boys to sleep and went into the kitchen to make coffee. I had knots in my stomach. I needed to speak to Andre; he always gave me the strength to overcome difficult situations. It was dark outside; I sat on the sofa with my coffee in hand and opened Facebook. As I scrolled through reading the many statuses people had posted the night before, I could feel the intense emotion building up inside me. I started to write.

"Let's do this, baby. We will ride together for the last time. I no longer need to have your back, but I know you will have mine for the rest of my life. Hold me up today as you always have. I love you."

Today I had to keep myself together. I had to make sure that Andre had the best send-off. This child of mine was unique. The love he had for me was shown every day. He appreciated me, and I loved him unconditionally. Never in my lifetime had I ever had to experience anything remotely like this. I had lost people I loved very much, but this was on a completely different level. I didn't know how to feel or act, and I didn't know how I would cope with what was to come; all I knew was that I had to get to the end of the day and survive it.

The morning moved slowly. I took my time to get dressed in the purple/blue dress I had brought to wear to represent my son's favourite colours and then organised the clothing for the boys so they could get ready. My husband and stepson were due to arrive soon. I had their trousers and shirts hanging and purple ties for the boys. Looking at the clothes hanging up in the bedroom felt so wrong. Everyone was getting dressed in suits to bury our Andre when we should be getting dressed for a celebration instead. I was pacing up and down, continuously checking the clock to keep myself busy. It was a tactic I had been using to distract myself from releasing all the painful emotions I was carrying inside. I took myself off to the garage, took a deep breath and pulled open the door. Laying on the floor of the garage were the flowers my friend and I spent many emotional nights putting together. I carried them one by one down to the driveway. The close family had arrived by now and were gathering outside. What a strange feeling as they all just stood there with tears rolling down their faces watching me carry the flowers out one at a time. Thinking back to that moment, I now realise they were amazed and shocked at how I behaved. It was weird behaviour; I see that now.

As I stood there looking at everyone, organising who was getting into what cars, around the corner came the hearse. The silence was deafening as the cars crept into the cul-de-sac and turned around before stopping outside the house. My baby boy lay inside the white coffin I had chosen for him. Draped over the coffin was the Arsenal flag, Andre's team. The funeral director got out of the car and greeted me, offering his condolences. He then took the instruction to place the flowers into the hearse. Everyone was staring at me as I continued to busy myself. When the back of the hearse was opened, I slid out the coffin, re-arranging the flag, and placed the flowers the way I wanted.

"I can do that for you", said the funeral director.

I looked at him and then continued with what I was doing. This was my son, after all, and I was capable of placing a few flowers and spreading out a flag over the coffin. Crazy behaviour. I don't know why I was behaving like this; maybe I was stuck in auto pilot. I couldn't stop this need to be in control. This would be the last thing I ever got to do for my son. There would be no more planning of birthdays or buying Christmas presents. I was no longer going to be able to clean his bedroom or drop him off at a mate's house, so I guess I was trying to savour every last moment left for me to do something for him. The funeral directors were confused and concerned. I could see it in their faces as they watched me carry out the work they were used to doing. It didn't matter to me that they had probably never seen a mother behave this way before; I just had to keep going. What would everyone have preferred, that I stood there bawling my eyes out.? Tears were not going to change the situation that I was dealing with. An unbelievable situation that I wouldn't wish on my worst enemies. All I knew at this moment was that I needed to keep going.

Andre's father was running exceptionally late. Late to his own son's funeral. My estranged husband was moaning about the lack of parental responsibility that he was showing and how unreliable he was; any opportunity to have a dig was something I was familiar with hearing. I just wanted him to shut up. Today was not the day to pick who had done what for whom. Today was a day about all the people who were a part of Andre's life coming together to say goodbye to the young man they had known and loved and to support each other through what was going to be one of the worst days of our lives He finally pulled up in his car. I could see the anguish on his face as he rushed to join us on the pavement. What a situation to arrive at. He wasn't like me and couldn't hide the loss he was feeling. It was written all over his face and oozing out with his body language. I think that, for the most part, it was his regrets for not having the father-son relationship with Andre that he could have had. He didn't know what to say, act or do to be the father in this situation. We started the final journey.

The first stop was Heathfield Vale. I requested that we drive past the house we had happily lived in as a family for one last time. From here, we would drive up to the street where Andre was found, known as 'The Flowers', where everyone found comfort in visiting for some strange reason. Here we would walk the length of the street just like he would have done that night, lay flowers, and stand in silence for one last time. From here, we would travel directly to the church in Selsdon for the service before finishing Andre's journey at Croydon Cemetery. Well, what can I say? In true Andre style, the plans I had methodically prepared with the funeral directors did not go the way I intended. I still laugh about it now because I could feel his presence so strong that morning; he clearly had different plans. I can't emphasise how much the Monks Hill community meant to Andre. That was his stomping ground, the place he loved to be the most. Even when he was out, he wasn't out of the estate. As we sat in the limousine behind the hearse, the first mistake was the driver driving straight past the road that we were supposed to turn down. I sat up in my seat to see what the confusion was about.

"Where is he going?" I asked our driver.

The cars came to a halt as they realised the mistake that they had made.

"We are so sorry", he continued., "We will have to reroute for you; please accept our apologies."

I couldn't stop smiling. I knew exactly what was going on here. It felt as though Andre was in total control. He was going to have things the way that he wanted. As the cars pulled off to enable us to enter the road from the right end, I realised straight away that this was going to mean that we would have to do a complete tour of the estate to get back to where we needed to be. I just smiled. Just imagine for one moment looking into the funeral car of a teenager that had been brutally murdered and seeing the mother of that child smiling from ear to ear. Well, that's what I was doing. Andre was getting his final tour around the area that he loved so much and on every doorstep was a member of the community out to witness his send-off.

We passed the Spar where I had dropped him off that night. Looking out of the window, I could picture him standing in front of the shop, smiling at me like he did on that terrible day. People were out, some wearing tee shirts with Andre's face on it. They looked shocked and saddened as we passed. We drove by the green telecoms box, which he sat on outside the flats. We passed the road that he had run down, then back past the community centre, and finally the green in the middle of the estate where the air ambulance had landed that evening. He was definitely in control of this minor mishap, but it felt right. The right journey, his last tour.

As we approached the church, it was the amount of people that I could see that contributed to the overwhelming feeling that I had growing deep down inside. It was a slow drive up the church's driveway where groups of people congregated outside waiting for Andre's arrival. Seeing my nephews and nieces standing by the church entrance had an instant emotional impact on me. Andre was the big cousin that they all looked up to him. He had always been the one they looked forward to seeing when he visited. Andre was silly. He would wrestle with them and bounce with them on the trampoline. Andre's passion for football was shared with the boys' cousins, and he would have them in the garden for hours coaching them and teaching them new tricks with the football. He would be so proud of the boys as they pursued their football careers and gained signings with premier league teams. Andre would have been bigging them up and making sure that everyone knew how proud of them he was.

The vicar of the church was outside to greet us. I hadn't confirmed pallbearers, but the boys wanted to carry the coffin into the church. How wrong did that feel? The younger brothers and cousins were going to take on the responsibility of carrying their beloved brother into the church. I looked at Ashley, fourteen years old, taking on the responsibility of leading his cousins into the church. As I continued to busy myself with the arrangements of who should stand where the vicar turned to me.

"Let me take it from here, Yemi", she said.

She could see that I was putting on an emotionally anxious act to stop myself from breaking down, but she also knew that it couldn't continue. I needed to let her lead the service; after all, that was her job. I looked at her in agreement, and we entered the church. I never expected to see so many people in the church. There must have been at least five hundred people in the congregation, with more standing at the back and down the aisles. So many familiar faces. I saw some regularly and others I hadn't seen in a while. Old people and young people all stood there watching as I followed the white coffin down the church aisle holding hands lightly with my youngest Amari.

As I walked, I turned my head from left to right, taking in all the different people who had turned out to support us on Andre's final journey. As I looked around, I could see tears, so many tears on so many faces.

"It's okay, don't cry", I said as I walked, following the coffin with my baby in it.

Stopping to hug people and console them before finally taking a seat at the front of the church. I cannot remember the entire service. I remember the order and who got up to speak because I had planned the whole thing. Since then, I have listened to the audio recording back in parts, but it is harrowing. Hearing myself and others speak about Andre with so much pain in their voices from their loss still chokes me up over five years later. Aside from me, Andre's former Head Teacher spoke honestly about the type of child Andre was at school. Everyone in the congregation who knew Andre could relate to what he was saying. Andre was a loveable rogue, and that never changed.

My sisters, Andre's aunties, spoke, and Ashley, Andre's little brother. There were also tributes read from Andre's Nan and cousins with the Eulogy being read so beautifully by Andre's big cousin. Everything everyone said was truthful and showed what an absolutely beautiful soul he really was. Andre's sister came to the front of the church, placing her hand on the beautiful white coffin before singing a song we had planned together and she had been practising. I don't think there was a dry eye in the church once she started. A talent that came from their father's side of the family. Andre could also sing, even though he didn't want anyone to know. I suppose he preferred rap, which was the influential culture of young people his age, but I loved hearing him sing, especially when he drew the deepness out of his voice to sing Oprah. He did this from time to time, a type of party trick, but I don't think he realised how powerful his voice really was.

After the service, we made our way to the cemetery. Lowering the coffin into the ground and saying prayers before the funeral directors approached me.

"Do you want us to fill in the grave once we have finished, or should we hand it over to the family?" the director asked me.

It's traditional in the black culture for family members to bury their own. To take the shovel and cover the coffin with every piece of earth that came from the space.

"Give me the shovel, please, no one else", I instructed.

Once one hundred white roses had been thrown on top of Andre's coffin by those that wanted, I tied up my hair, put my welly boots on and made my way to the top of the pile of earth to the side of where my boy now laid. I took a deep breath and looked out at the crowd of people watching. With the strength I had left, I dug into the earth and threw the first pile down on my baby. It hit the coffin with a thud; a sound that I have and always will hate. I didn't stop. Shovel after shovel, I tossed the earth through the air into the hole. I could feel my legs trembling. I had never done anything like this before. It wasn't bravery or having to prove any points. It was simple, he was my baby. I carried him for nine months as he grew inside my body; I protected him from harm. I gave birth to him, brought him home in my arms and raised him solo during some of the most difficult times of my late teens and early twenties. Andre was a year older than I was when I had him. What did I really know about anything? I hadn't even really experienced any sort of life at this point; becoming a teenage mum made me have to grow up very quickly, but I rose to the challenge. I was at the end of his life, covering him with earth, and he hadn't even started to experience half of the things I had at his age. There was no legacy. He never had the chance to have a serious relationship, experience falling in love, having a home of his own or his own child. This was so wrong, but again I was going to take responsibility as his mother to ensure that I did everything I could on this final day, 19th October 2016.

Shortly after, as I started to run out of energy, others joined me in the task. Ashley, Andre's dad, uncles, and cousins came to ensure that, as a family, we could complete the job of covering our loved one. Watching your fourteen-year-old throw dirt over his brother, the boy he loved and looked up to, was heart-wrenching. I was not sure how we would be able to get over what had happened to us as a family. Ashley wanted to do his bit. Like me, he felt he was obliged to do whatever needed to be done to give Andre the best send-off. He wanted to be part of everything we were doing, and I tried to include him as much as possible but also tried to shield and protect him from all the details of what happened that day. As Ashley dug into the red earth, which resembled lumps of wet clay, he flicked the shovel. The dirt flew into the hole, and so did the shovel. We can look back now and laugh about the situation. Ashley tries to mask the innocent mistake as a plot to leave Andre the shovel to dig himself out if needed. It didn't deter him; once the shovel was retrieved, he pulled up his sleeves and continued with the task.

Amari worried me. Throughout the entire day, he remained almost silent. He didn't speak at all, just followed along with wherever we went. As we all worked to cover the grave, Amari stood on the edge of the graveside, watching everything everyone was doing. He had gone from being a happy, clever, talented eight-year-old to throwing tantrums and screaming as if the pain was too severe for him. The last week he had gone silent, and today was no different. I looked at him standing with toes to the edge, peering down inside the grave. I feared how this would change him. Amari and Andre were so similar and incredibly close. They had birthdays four days apart, and Andre doted on him. This had to affect him, but I was praying that he would be able to bounce back at his young age. Only time would tell.

At one point, I looked up and noticed a group of Andre's friends gathered on the pathway, slightly away from what we were doing. I understand that young people may find the whole event of burying their friend alien. For some of them, this may have been the first time they had experienced the loss of someone they loved, especially being in such a tragic way, but I found the way that they were behaving peculiar. I approached them; this wasn't right. This was their friend, after all. Their ride or die, the ones that were supposed to love him and be there whatever the situation.

"Come and help", I said to the boys. Bradley in particular.

He obliged but hesitantly. As Bradley stood on the pile of the earth beneath him with the shovel in his hand, I watched him freeze. The sweat started to pour from his head, and he looked like a rabbit caught in headlights. This bothered me. Okay, they were young, and this was hard for them, but placing some of the earth on the boy, whom they referred to as their brother, wasn't that hard. I thought he would have wanted to do this, but on reflection the following day, I felt sorry for him. Maybe I was asking too much. Just because I was strong enough to do this didn't mean that everyone else was.

The rest of the evening went well. There was food, drink, and music. Storytelling and meaningful conversations. Some drank more than others. What else was left to do but sing, dance, celebrate Andre's short life and wash the emotions away with a strong drink? I was exhausted. All the preparations, waiting, and finally getting to the dreaded day were affecting me the more the day went on. My strength was diminishing, but I now had to deal with the behaviour of my very drunk husband. He couldn't accept that our marriage was over; it had been over for a long time, years. He just hadn't come to terms with it. If he had been able to put his emotions to the side about our relationship and support the boys and me throughout this ordeal, we could have tried to build our relationship again, but he just couldn't do that. Whilst all my focus was on Andre, the murder, the funeral, the trial and getting some stability back for the boys, he was trying to work out how we could get our marriage back on track. That was the furthest thing from my mind at the time. All I needed was support and someone to lean on when I was having my weak days to help me back up, and that wasn't going to be him.

The funeral ended with a bang. I knew it wouldn't be long before the husband I had been dealing with for the past few years would rear its ugly head. After the wake, a mixture of drunkenness and emotions raised out of him in a public spectacle that left me trembling. We all piled into the cars to return to my house. As I snuggled up next to Amari on the back seat of Andre's school friend's car, waiting for him to drop me home safely, my husband approached the car pulling the door open.

"You know what you are, don't you" he slurred under the liquor he had been consuming for most of the day.

I knew that he was about to start an argument; I had witnessed this behaviour on many occasions before, so I knew what it looked like. Why would he do this today and in front of the children? After hurling abuse at me, he slammed the car door so hard the force could have knocked me out the other side.

I'm not going to talk about what happened after this because I don't think it would be fair on all involved. Needless to say, it wasn't nice, and I wish my husband had been able to control his emotions because this just contributed to everything that continued to happen moving forward. The need to get so far away from someone as soon as possible motivated all my decisions after this. These were life-changing not only for me but also for the boys.

CHAPTER THIRTEEN
THE ESCAPE

The next few months were a blur. From August 16th until October 19th, I had purpose, a reason to get up every morning and to carry on. I kept myself busy with the planning of the funeral and the daily updates of the investigation into my baby's murder but now that was over. The only schedule I had was to get up in the morning to drop the boys to school and then to be back for 3pm to collect them. What happened between those times were never planned and for the first time in a long time I had no real drive to my life anymore. The doctor had prescribed me with anti-depressant tablets and sleeping pills to help me to relax at night, but I just couldn't bring myself to take them. That may have been easier, it may have helped but I was scared that I wouldn't be able to stop taking them when the time came, but worse than that I was scared that I would no longer be able to feel. I needed to feel the loss of my son. I wasn't sure if I would be able to feel the emotions that I was expected to feel if I topped myself up on medication every day. I had to feel him, however unbearable the pain was going to be I needed to experience it, to live it, to deal with my loss. I hadn't been eating properly for a long time and I had lost a considerable amount of weight. I was worried about how I was neglecting my health and how my poor decision making would affect me in the future.

One Saturday afternoon as I stood in the kitchen in Andre's grey dressing gown and Nike sliders which I had brought him for what I never knew would be his last Christmas, I was washing up and clearing away the takeaway boxes from the food brought for the boys the night before. I had a pile of clean cups and dishes on the draining board and a teenage son moaning in my ear.

"Please mum, can I go and meet my friends?", Ashley was begging for about the one hundredth time that afternoon.

"No", I responded.

What did he not get about me not wanting him to go over to the Monks Hill Estate? I just couldn't fathom why he would want to keep going back to the place where his brother had been chased through the streets and slayed in front of the whole community. I didn't know who to trust. My gut instincts were driving me crazy, and he just wouldn't shut up going on about it. He didn't see any danger in being back on the estate, but I couldn't help but think that was exactly what Andre had said a few months ago. It felt bad enough as a mother that I hadn't protected my first-born son and I couldn't help but to think that losing one son was a tragedy, but could you imagine what it would be like if I lost another.

I was trying to explain to him hoping that he would be mature enough to listen and understand where I was coming from, but he wouldn't. I felt for him, both of them. We had no internet access in the house, so PlayStation and Netflix were out of the question, plus they had a paranoid mum who was keeping them hidden from everyone including the ice cream man. The battle that I was going through internally coupled with the pressure that I was being put under by my teenage son was too much and I flipped. In a mad rage I cleared the draining board of every cup, plate and saucer that was there. The more I smashed the more I wanted to smash. The sound of the crockery hitting the floor was so satisfying but I was in an out-of-control rage. As I turned around, I saw the boys and my niece standing in the doorway shielding for cover to not be hit from the flying objects that I was hurling around the kitchen. Then I stopped. I couldn't do this anymore. How was I supposed to continue living doing menial tasks such as washing up, without a care in the world when my son's body was decomposing in the ground and there was nothing, I could do about it? I grabbed my car keys and left the house.

Some time had passed, and I could hear a ringing sound in the distance. As the ringing continued my mind slowly returned to my body, I regained consciousness. There I was stood in the pouring rain still wearing Andre's grey dressing gown and sliders with my two feet on top of Andre's grave. The ringing from my phone which was on the passenger seat of my car which I had driven right up next to Andre's grave and got out leaving the door wide open was bringing me back to reality. As I came around, I noticed several other people in the cemetery visiting their loved ones looking at me in disbelief. No one approached me. They must have thought that I was completely crazy. I mean I don't blame them; I was drenched through, sobbing and didn't even know how I had got where I was. I walked back to the car. Several missed calls from my sister who had been informed by her daughter that I had left the house and she was obviously concerned about me. I was concerned about me. I had been trying to be so strong for so long, but it was all getting on top of me. I couldn't help but think that they should have taken me too. Andre was all alone, and I didn't like that feeling. I could have laid on top of his grave and fallen asleep just to feel close to my son. I moved my focus to my other sons and made the decision to drive back home where I knew that they still needed me. I often had loads of thoughts running through my head. Bad ones. Thoughts of getting into my car and driving it through a brick wall or off the edge of a bridge. The only thing that stopped me was the boys having to deal with another loss. They were just about coping day by day with the loss of Andre, how could I then leave them too. That would definitely break them and would have been so selfish of me. I needed to shake that feeling, I was being strong for them and everyone else, who was being strong for me?

There were other days like this one, days when I just couldn't stop crying. I would go to sleep after dropping the boys to school and wish that Andre would come to me to tell me that he was doing alright and that I didn't need to worry. I felt like I needed to escape from the life I was currently living. Something to take my mind off the way that I was feeling. I tried to return to work but my hypervigilance in such a noisy environment was doing more harm than good. Lunch times were the worst. I would lock myself away from the students because every scream, bang or screech would send my heart racing. I tried to be there for a couple of days and then stopped. I wasn't ready. As much as I appreciated having my colleagues around me there were just too many memories inside the building that I just wasn't ready to deal with.

I found comfort in my DJ friend. He just seemed to know what to say and do to make me feel safe and the times that I spent with him helped me with my healing. Being separated from my husband, having to support and parent the boys single handed and having to be careful about what I put on my family led me to form a greater bond with him. It wasn't that my family were not there to support me because they were. If I needed to have one of them around or have a chat on the phone or have support with something, they would have dropped whatever to help me. It was me. I couldn't be vulnerable in front of them because them seeing me in a bad way made them worse and I knew my mum was already struggling so much to manage herself on a daily basis. I felt responsible for her, and I know that she wanted to be responsible for helping me, but I have always been the strongest in our family and felt it was my duty to continue that way.

He was able to support me. He would talk to me every day and check to see if I had slept and eaten. He would listen to me wail down the phone when I was weak and share words of wisdom with me to help me through how I was feeling in the moment. He always seemed to say the right things to make me smile again and at that time he was just what I needed. A couple of times a week after I had dropped the boys to school, I would take the thirty-minute drive to his house. It is hard to explain but being out of Croydon helped me to settle, to feel safe. I would get to the door, and he would be stood there to greet me with empathy written on his face. He made me feel safe.

"You look tired", he would say.

I was always tired. He would tuck me up in bed and sit with me until I fell asleep. When I woke, he would make lunch and those days when I didn't have the strength to eat, he would feed me to ensure that I had something inside me, to keep me going. We would talk things through and when I cried, he would hold me in his strong arms and simply say "hush".

That is all I needed. To be somewhere else being looked after. It was never my intention to start a relationship with him but the more time that we spent together the more my feelings grew. I often asked myself if Andre would approve and I knew he would. He would want me to have someone to support me when he was not there to do so.

"Just be happy mum", he used to say to me. "I don't care what you do as long as you are happy".

Andre meant it whole heartedly. He knew the single mummy and the married mummy and even though marriage changes you, he didn't like the person that I had become. I was on edge, not allowed to be myself. I was depressed. I used to come home from work and go straight to bed to avoid arguments. Don't get me wrong sometimes he used to pull me up if I was in the wrong. He wasn't biased just because I was his mum. I brought him up like that, no wrong and strong, so if I was wrong, he would make me know.

I was vulnerable, but that didn't mean that he was taking advantage of this. I knew exactly what I was doing and why I was doing it. If anything, it was probably me making demands on his time and he had found himself in a position of responsibility. He wanted me to be okay. We had known each other for fifteen plus years and although I was going through the worst experiences of my entire life, he had a way of making me feel able to cope with whatever life was throwing at me. I was probably the one that was taking advantage of him and when I needed to escape, he was the one that I wanted by my side.

I had a murder trial looming. By February 2017 I would be in court everyday fighting for justice for my son. I had been pre warned that this would be a very exhausting experience, so I had it in my head that I needed a break before it started. One day when I was getting ready to leave his house, he was sat in the living room, and I posed the question.

"Let's go to Jamaica before the trial", I asked him.

He looked at me, a bit bemused. I think that he thought that I was joking about and was just verbalising my inner feelings.

"Why not", he said.

I left and went home and that evening I scrolled the internet looking at holidays to Jamaica. I loved Jamaica. I first visited Negril in 2015 with my sister-in-law Mandy. It was part of our trip to visit Sam's grave and check in on her family. I remember waking up in Jamaica the first morning after I arrived and feeling like I had woken up in paradise. It was dark by the time we arrived at the hotel so the following morning to the sound of the cockerel's and the waves of the sea bashing the beach I opened the patio door and made my way out onto the balcony. At 6am in the morning the sun was beating down on my skin. The smell of food cooking and reggae music playing in the background I just knew that this was a country that I was going to fall in love with.

We had only spent a week in Jamaica, but it had been the longest, best week of my life. Laying on a sun lounger on the beach, talking to the locals, shopping in the markets and swimming in the sea was some of the best experiences of my life. Now I was experiencing the worst times of my life I couldn't think of anywhere better to be than Jamaica to recover and prepare myself before the trial. I sent him a WhatsApp.

"So, if we can get the money together do you want to take a break?" I asked.

"And stay where hun?", he responded.

"Negril on the beach?".

I loved Negril but to be honest it didn't really matter where we stayed as long as I was out of the country and in the sun and able to get some peace. It had been nonstop since Andre was murdered. The media had gone crazy always a story and a write up with everyone trying to have their say and opinions. I was getting fed up with it. I would send myself crazy listening to the readers putting their two pence worth in without even knowing anyone who was involved. I would go to the supermarket and people would stop to speak to me. The strangest time is when strangers would just hug me. No warning or conversation but just grab you for a cuddle. I couldn't even have normal conversations without watching the tears welling up in somebody's eyes. I appreciated the level of sympathy that was being shown but my life wasn't private anymore and being in Jamaica would take away the constant attention so I could properly rest before facing the next round. We talked for a further few days, fantasising about being together in a country we both loved before I took the plunge and booked the flights and hotel. Seven nights all-inclusive and only 87 days before we left.

I once again had something to plan, prepare and look forward too. This time, not like the preparations that I had needed to make for Andre but something to uplift me and give me hope. I had to buy new summer clothes and organise who would look after the boys whilst I was away and make certain that this was going to be the escape that I needed even if just for a short period of time. I had the holiday app and the countdown clock which I was allowed to send him a screen shot of once a week. We were both excited, I had never been on holiday with a man before not abroad anyway, so this was going to be a first. I think it was a first for him too. He had been away with his family but not with a woman, this was something that we were going to share together, and I couldn't wait. Not everyone was excited for me. Some people couldn't understand why we were going away together and why I hadn't asked a girlfriend or family member to go with me. Well, that was simple. I was trying to escape. I didn't want to take anyone away with me that was going to keep me in the same state of mind that I was in at home. I knew he would uplift me and also keep my mind off of everything that I had been dealing with and that is what I wanted. I could have gone on holiday with my boys, but I needed a break, I didn't want to be responsible for anyone. I wanted to have someone who made me feel safe who could be responsible for me, and it worked.

Between planning the escape to Jamaica and getting the first Christmas out of the way, I received more shocking news which didn't only place another level of fear into my life but also made me feel completely let down.

"Do you have that phone Yemi?", Katy asked me on a late evening phone call.

Nothing that she was saying to me made any sense. The only phone that Andre had was the one that Police had in their possession. Katy explained to me that one of the phone numbers that I had given to her on the night of Andre's murder was still actively making and receiving calls. During the investigation Police had been collecting the call data for all numbers which had called Andre on the days before his murder, calls taken on the day and any calls that he made. This was to try to piece together all those who were in custody and work out how they knew where Andre was on that day.

"When we went up to Kent, he gave his spare phone to his friend", I told her.

"Thank you and please do not call the phone", Katy responded.

I didn't know what all this meant but I was sure that it somehow put Andre's friends in the mix. Maybe my gut feeling about their involvement and their strange behaviour wasn't all in my head after all. The escape that I needed couldn't come quick enough. I needed a break from everything that was going on because it was beginning to drive me crazy.

Whilst I was away, I thought about Andre every minute of every day. I could picture him sat on the decking by the beach with his grey tracksuit bottoms rolled up to his knees and his t-shirt hanging around his neck with one arm in and one out. If I had one regret, it would have been not having the opportunity to take him abroad one more time. I had taken Andre on a family holiday to Greece when he was four and it was those photos of that holiday that I enjoyed looking at now. That was a great holiday but after that holiday and having more children the money was never available to take the boys away. Ashley and Amari had never left the country so I made a vow there and then that I would take them away after the trial. This break was for me, to get some of my strength back to fight the next battle but they deserved to escape too so I would have to make that happen. I was relaxed, smiling, and sleeping through the night without having any nightmares. I had no responsibilities for an entire week and although I checked in on the boys every day and they called me when they wanted too, I could eat, sleep, smoke, and drink when I wanted. There was not one night for the seven nights that I was away that I woke up sweating, reliving the nightmare of August 16th in my dreams. I didn't once jump out of my sleep with the feeling that someone was in the room wanting to murder me. I stopped laying awake all night trying to figure out what every little sound was and whether I needed to investigate it to make sure it wasn't a threat to my life. He made me feel safe and I could relax knowing he was there laying next to me as I slept. I think that this was probably the only time throughout this entire ordeal that I was able to keep the demons and the overthinking that was constantly in my head at bay. I didn't think that it would be possible for me to find any happiness ever again, but I was happy in Jamaica with him. If I could have just stayed there and not returned to England, I would have been relieved but that definitely was not a possibility.

One day we took a trip to Dunn's River Falls. It is a tourist attraction, a must do, if you visit Jamaica. We had a great time on the tour, climbing the falls with the water beating against us, working together hand in hand pulling each other up and supporting one another so not to fall. We took the backwards fall into the waters linked arm in arm, together we hit the water before coming back up to the surface giggling like two love struck teenagers. It was the perfect day until the coach journey back. The traffic was slow, crawling along the wide road. There were no pavements just grass verges. It became apparent very quickly that we had been caught up in some type of accident that had happened up ahead. The coach was hot so a few of us hopped off to walk alongside the coach as it crawled up the street. As we walked and smoked, ahead we could see a commotion. People walking towards us who had passed the incident already described what they saw as a road traffic accident with a fatality. We hopped back onto the coach as the traffic started to move more quickly and as we approached the scene of the accident there on the side of the road was the body of a young man who had been killed in the collision. Police had covered his body with a plastic sheet and all I could see was his feet sticking out from beneath it. It took my breath away. All emotions of Andre's death came racing back to me. I tried in my mind to separate the two incidents, but I just couldn't. Seeing another young person laying on the street dead was dragging me into an emotional turmoil. I instantly started sobbing. I was sat on a bus full of strangers in a swimsuit and a throwover sobbing my heart out. The tears were streaming down my face, and I was struggling to breath. Everyone on the bus must have thought that it was an extreme over reaction to what we had all just witnessed but he knew better. I didn't need to tell him he picked up how I was reacting and knew that this was directly linked to the trauma and emotions that I was carrying for Andre. He sat next to me, real close so that I could feel his heart beating and he held me tight.

'Hush', he said. And that was all he ever had to say to.

CHAPTER FOURTEEN
THE TRIAL WITNESSES AND EVIDENCE

It was over, back to reality with a bump. Preparations for court were underway and I was receiving regular updates from our FLO about what to expect. February 13th, 2017, saw the first day of the trial. I was not allowed to attend. It was one of the biggest days of this case and I had to stay at home because I was to appear later as a witness. My sisters attended so that they could give me regular updates of what was happening.

ANDRE'S TRIAL UPDATE

Broadcast one
Today in court the jury were selected but the defence team asked for extra days so that they can review new evidence that had been received.

Tomorrow – The Jury will be sworn in
Wednesday – Opening Statements will be given at 10am
Please continue to pray and keep us in your thoughts.......

Broadcast two
February 15th
Today in court the opening statements were given.
Tomorrow – I will be giving evidence at 10am alongside Charlie.
Court starts at 10am in Court 8 and I am expecting it to last all day.
Please continue to pray and keep us in your thoughts.......

Broadcast three
February 20th
Today in court there were three witnesses that came to give evidence. They all did really well and none of them were friends of Andre's, so it was good to hear what happened from an unbiased point of view. The defence barristers are trying really hard to unsettle them and make them feel confused, but they stood their ground.
Tomorrow they will continue to introduce key witnesses which are being seen in order to show how the chase happened.

Today was hard because they revealed that Andre had been hit by Lonergan's car and although the witnesses suggest that the car run over his legs, I'm not sure that this is true. I know he was hit but it probably caused injury to his knees which we know about, but I don't know about any broken bones.

The trial continues tomorrow at 10am in Court 8.

Please continue to pray and keep us in your thoughts.......

As I'm shattered.

Broadcast 4
February 21st

Today in court we started with the young man from yesterday who saw Andre appear from the alleyway being chased by three youths. He also saw the car parked up waiting.

We then heard from a paramedic who also saw Andre run into the alleyway followed by three boys.

Both these witnesses saw knives.

Finally, we heard from a man that was buying a vehicle. He witnessed the car parked badly near where Andre was found and also saw what he described as four boys kicking and beating something on the floor which we know was Andre. He also heard him screaming. He went around the car and left the estate but shortly after found that the car was in front of him driving at excessive speed.

Some evidence again today which ties all suspects to the scene.

Barristers didn't really have much to argue today.

Tomorrow more key witnesses who saw the attack take place.

The trial continues tomorrow at a later time of 10:45am in Court 8.

Please continue to pray and keep us in your though.

Quick update

I have been advised that no family or friends should go in the public gallery tomorrow.

I will keep you updated when I know more.

I didn't write anymore broadcasts after that one.

As I travelled home on the train every evening, I had been giving everyone an update of the accounts of the day but the more that the trial went on and the more information that I was hearing the harder it was for me to focus on anything.

I was emotional, I thought I knew what happened to Andre on that day until I actually listened to the evidence that was being presented. I would get home every night, run a hot bath and lay in it until the water went cold. More often than not I would empty and top it up with hot water. I had to do this because I had to mask the tears that I was crying so that the boys wouldn't worry.

Witness One – The lady taking driving lessons

This witness had been on a driving lesson and had just pulled up on the side of the road having a conversation with her instructor before the lesson finished. She said that through the rear-view mirror she saw a man that was running fast like he was trying to get away from someone. As he passed the car that she was sitting in she saw Andre stumble, trip over falling onto his front. The witness described seeing his upper half on the pavement with his legs still in the road.

"From behind him, almost immediately, came a white car travelling fast. It looked as if it had come from the same direction as the running man. Before he was able to get back to his feet, I saw the car deliberately turn towards him and run over his legs" she said.

Tears filled my eyes. My baby had been hunted by a pack of wolves and it looked like they were willing to go to any lengths to get him. I put my head in my hands as I tried to fight back the tears. I looked to my left where the defendants were sitting in the dock only a meter away. Lonergan sat facing the front with no expression on his face. It was him that she was talking about. I wondered what he was thinking and how he could just sit there so calmly knowing that he had contributed to my son's death and the pain that we as a family were enduring.

"Very shortly after the running man was run over, I saw three more men who also appeared to be chasing him. They came running around the corner from the same direction as the running man and the car, and by the time the running man had got up and run towards the alley, the three chasing them were only a metre or so behind him" she continued.

"I could see that all three of the chasing men had knives in their hands".

The witness describes hearing a male voice shouting, "Allow me, Allow me!".

That was Andre. I had a hundred and one thoughts racing through my mind. Did they catch him in the alley? Did they stab him there and then he ran until he dropped? My heart was racing, anger was boiling up inside of me. I really did not want to look at them. How dare they behave like that to someone else's child. My baby must have been petrified!

The witness's story didn't end there, she was able to describe what each one of the defendants looked like and the types of weapons that each carried. She described the car and what she heard after she had gone inside. I felt so grateful for her evidence. She was only young herself and I know that it must have taken an enormous amount of courage to come to court and testify at a murder trial.

Witness Two – A local teen

The evidence that this witness gave was vital. It showed that the defendants were planning to find Andre and his friends in the lead up to his murder. He had seen the defendants on the estate on August 14th, two days before they came back and killed my son. On this night they were calling out for Andre's friend threatening to kill him. The witness shared that he had seen them filming and had also seen knives on that night.

"I saw Andre talking to a man. The man was telling him that some boys were up on the estate the day before and they were looking for Andre and his friends and he should go home before they see him", he said.

"Andre didn't reply although I think he listened to him as he said 'bye' and started to walk off"

This is when I knew that Andre had worked out that something was wrong. Why didn't he just call me or leave straight away? I was angry at him but also angry at myself. I shouldn't have left; I should have waited for his friends to arrive that way I would have been able to have kept him safe.

The witness describes how about ten minutes later he could hear shouting outside. As he looked out, he could see Andre being chased by boys with knives.

Witness Three – The woman at the window

There were several witnesses but what the third witness had to say shocked me the most. She had a clear view of the final moments before the defendants fled the scene. Her evidence continues to traumatise me.

"The male fell with his head closest to the building. Two of the chasing males were kicking the male on the floor in the upper torso area and the third was standing back. They did this more than once, maybe three or four times. The male on the floor was curled up in the foetal position. One of the males then kicked the male on the floor in the head. He did this three times making the male on the floor's head roll. The kicks were quite forceful. I think the post-mortem will show his head was a pulp as he lost consciousness and everything. When he was kicked in the head his body moved outwards from the foetal position he had been in" she said.

What was I actually listening to? Stabbing Andre so many times, threatening him with a gun and then kicking him in the head when he is laying on the floor bleeding to death and unconscious. I could no longer hold the tears back. I didn't want the jury to see my emotional responses to what I was hearing but I could no longer fight what was happening to me.

"Do you need to go outside?" Katy asked.

"No", I shook my head.

I was going to listen to every last piece of evidence that was given. I needed to hear it all. I had been imagining for months what could have happened. Trying to piece together all the information that I had heard from different people, but this was the first time that I was hearing first-hand accounts from the actual people who witnessed it. As hard as this was listening to them give their accounts, I needed to know. I thought that what I was imagining was over exaggerated, but the truth of the matter was that the truth was a thousand times worse. The evidence that came in the next few days and weeks only got worse. For the first time I had a clearer understanding of what had happened on that day. Each witness gave their accounts, but it was a female witness who had also lived on the estate whose evidence tore me up inside. Her evidence described events unfolding that sounded like they belonged in a horror movie. She was clearly traumatised by everything that she had seen. Her voice was fragile, and you could hear her trembling as she gave evidence via video link. She had left the country because of what she had witnessed. Like me she had needed to escape but I am again so thankful for the detail that she shared and the courage that she mustered up in order to deliver what can only be described as a callous plight to murder my boy.

Witness Four – Women in the flats

"As Andre reached the pathway the male swung the pole and struck Andre across the right side of his head just above his ear with such force that I don't know how Andre managed it, but he seemed to just stagger a little and then recover and continue running", she said.

Her voice was croaky which I knew was because she was trying to hold back her tears. I leaned over and whispered to my sister.

"He got hit in the face?".

She looked at me in dismay but didn't answer. Later on, that day she explained to me that when we had visited the mortuary, she had noticed that there was blood on the pillow.

She thought that he had an injury to his face which is why they had positioned him the way that they did when we visited. Why didn't I notice that? I was staring at him wishing him to wake, how did I not know that he had injuries to his face. My sister didn't want to upset me, so she kept it to herself. The witness continued.

"It was at this point that I saw the disturbing expression on the male's face. A look of pure joy as if he liked what he had done, and it was at this point that I noticed that his eyeballs were yellow"

Everyone including the members of the Jury turned to look at the four defendants sitting in the dock. It was undeniable. Mukasa sat there with a look of ugly on his face, scruffy hair, and yellow eyeballs. I knew of him and had heard Andre and his friends mention him in conversations especially after the first shooting. Andre referred to him by a nick name 'Glare' and now I knew why. He seemed to glare at you with discoloured eyes. I took a deep breath. What the witness was saying was true, but her evidence only got harder to listen to.

"What scared me the most was that I could see fear in Andre's eyes. Andre ran followed closely by the three males. One was holding a handgun in his hand, but he no longer had the pole. I lost sight of them", she said.

So not only did they bring knives to attack they also had a pole and a gun. What type of crazy, psycho people were these? All sat in the dock trying to look like butter wouldn't melt in their mouths. I knew at this point that they were bang to rights with the level of evidence that was linking them to my son's murder. All four of them might have well pleaded guilty and cut their losses. There could be no way that they could get away with this.

"Quite literally just after they went out of sight, no more than a few seconds later, I heard Andre scream a sequence of about four or five loud 'Arghs', each one getting shallower. His voice will never leave me for the rest of my life". She finished.

I could hear her voice break as she held back a sob. I felt incredibly sorry that she had to see and hear such things. Recalling what she had witnessed was clearly hard for her and as Andre's mother who hadn't witnessed the actually attack, I could only imagine with the level of pain that I was feeling, how this was affecting her. I needed answers. How many injuries did Andre actually have? His interim death certificate stated that he died from two stab wounds to the left side of his body.

Now I've heard that he was smacked around the face with a pole and with four to five screams I'm guessing that would collate to the same amount of stab injuries. I spoke to our FLO, and she agreed to show me the evidence book that had been compiled for use in court that showed the details of the injuries to Andre's body. She was concerned that if I saw them, I would not react well, and it could really damage me mentally. I needed to see them so that I knew what I was dealing with before they used them in the court room so the next morning we sat down together, and I was handed the book of images to look through.

As I turned the pages of the book there were images after images of the damages that were caused to his petite body that night, I sat shaking my head, holding back the tears.

- Seven Stab injuries to the left side of his back.
- Four were of significant depth
- Two had penetrated the lung to a depth of 10cm
- Four injuries to his upper left arm
- One slash wound which exposed muscle and tissue
- One passed completely through the arm for 9cm's
- Two wounds to the chest
- Injuries to the head and face
- Three puncture wounds to the scalp.
- Injuries to the left ear
- Injuries to the left side of the neck
- Patterned marks on the left cheek.

I sat there looking at each of the images running my fingers delicately across the pages. Trying to make sense of how cruel these four boys had been. What could possibly have hyped them up so much that they caused such injuries to one person who was defenceless and not even attempting to fight back? Andre also had several cuts to his hands that were described as defensive wounds. My baby was trying to defend himself with his hands and was attempting to try and grab the blade of the knife as it was lunged towards him. I felt extremely sad. I was told that the injuries that had been put in the book were actual photographs of the injuries that were on Andres body and that they had been super imposed onto a body image that wasn't his.

I was one hundred percent sure that the body in the book was Andre's. I was his mother after all. I recognised his hands, torso, legs, chest, and head shape. In the images Andre had a shaved head. It was only now that it dawned on me that all his hair would have been shaved off to reveal the injuries that were on his scalp. My child was stabbed in the head three times. Who does such things? All I knew at this point was that the Jury needed to find them all guilty and lock them away and throw away the key. He would have been mortified having a fully shaven head. Andre had gone through a phase when he started secondary school of having long hair of which I had to plait every weekend. It was hard work to manage his hair which was of a very tight curl afro texture. After about a year and a bit of washing, blow drying and braiding, I created a scenario that I wasn't proud of but at the time felt necessary. As I stood combing through Andre's hair and began making the partings on his scalp, I decided to tell him that he had head lice. Immediately without even having to continue the lie he decided that the hair needed to go there and then. I was never able to tell him the truth about the lice situation but on visiting his grave one day I felt compelled to confess what I had done and ask him to forgive me. I know that he would have laughed at me but what I would give now to just have a lock of his hair to feel once more.

Seeing the images made me want to vomit. They were far worse than I had ever anticipated, and this is where I think my PTSD started. I would go to bed at night and relive the entire attack as if I had witnessed it myself. I would be able to see all the places that he had been stabbed and the blood pouring out of his body. I could hear the noises that he was making, and picture close up the look on the murderers faces as they took satisfaction from what they were achieving.

As the trial continued there were more and more witnesses that were able to help make sense of what happened on that day. There was the local man who watched from across the road to where Andre fell to his fate. The man who had been on the estate to collect a car and had notice the white car parked badly in the street as he was driving out. The boy who knew Andre and the boys that were attacking him who was able to identify them.
The people in their car who witnessed the getaway and the disposal attempt of the murder weapons tossed from the car window. They were supposed to go over a wall never to be seen again but fortunately they landed on the pavement and were recovered quickly by Police. The weapons linked DNA to Andre and the defendants, and this find was key evidence in ensuring that they were each linked to his death. Every single one of them as the prosecution explained had worked as a tactical team and every single one of them played a part in that final outcome. The witness that touched me the most was the women who came to Andre's aid to try and keep him alive.

Witness Five – Lady dressed in white

"I was holding his hand", she said.

"I asked him what his name was, and he said, Andre. I asked him how old he was, he said 19 and then he asked me to get his mum", she said.

Hearing this broke me. He was dying on the ground and was asking for me. Then I felt a sudden pang of anger raising up inside of me. I got there, I was at the scene before he went to the hospital and before he died, and I wasn't able to see him again. Why didn't Police let me go to my boy. This thought began to really bother me. I get that he was in a bad way, and they needed to carry out some procedures on him that would have not been a good experience for me to have witnessed. I also fully understand that his level of injuries would have shocked me however I think that I am strong enough to have been able to have got my head into a stable enough place to have dealt with what was happening. Members of the public whom he didn't know, even though I will be forever grateful that they were there to help him and even give him some comfort in his worst moment but that could have been me too.

During cross examination the defence challenged this witness's evidence as she had explained that the knives that were used to stab Andre had been big.

"Did you see knives then?", the prosecution challenged.

"No", the women answered
"So, tell me, how do you know how big they were then? Surely you cannot make a judgement about this if you never actually saw any knives", they argued.

They were really trying to challenge and unbalance her and suggest that the evidence that she was giving was not factual. Her response left them unable to challenge and me with my mouth open.

"I didn't have to see the knives", she said, "I saw the holes in Andre's body", she continued to explain. "I was able to put my whole hand inside to try and pack the wounds and stop the bleeding, so I know that the knives that were used had to be big".

I question everyday if Andre knew that I was there. Did he know that I had jumped in the car and raced there to be by his side? Did he know that I was on the other side of those red blankets that were being help up to shield us all from the work that was being carried out? Did he know that I followed him all the way to the hospital in the Police car as he rode in the ambulance in front of me? I hope he knew because I question every single day if I had been able to hold his hand and kiss his face would it have made a difference and made him keep fighting for life. Would he have gone quicker, peacefully if he knew that I was there, or would he have fault harder? He put up a fight alright, over three hours before he finally gave in. Was he waiting for me? These thoughts kill me and even as I write these words on the page my throat gains a lump in it and my eyes are full of tears. I really hope he didn't know what was happening.

CHAPTER FIFTEEN
THE TRIAL DEFENDENTS AND THEIR FAMILIES

Listening to the prosecution strategically putting forward their case was so draining. The witness statements were so powerful and gave so much detail it was very difficult for the defending barristers to argue the case. Very limited challenge was coming from any of the four barristers that were representing the defendants. The day that they brought the weapons out in court was a really tough day. They were all sealed in evidence containers and were passed around for the jury to look at. I held the knife that killed my son. As I looked inside the weapon cylinder that the knife was enclosed in, I felt the pain all through my body. It was as if I was being cut from the inside out. I tried to not have eye contact with any of the defendants throughout the case. I didn't want to look at them, I didn't want them to see any pain in my face. They didn't deserve that at all. They had taken enough from me already and I was going to continue to keep my head up and my dignity in tacked.

The way that we were seated in the court room was really messed up. This is something that I raised later when I went to meet the Head Judge for Tea. As you entered the court room through the doors, situated to the left were four chairs. This is where we were sat throughout the entire trial. Along the same wall was the dock where the defendants sat. That was so close to us, the victim's family. When the defendants began giving evidence, they actually come out of a door that was situated next to my seat and walked past me to get to the stand. As I sat there and the dock door opened, I had to use every piece of strength that I had inside my body to not jump out of that seat and choke one of them to death. I know two wrongs don't make a right, but I didn't want to see any of them let alone hear their voices. I felt angry as they brushed past my knees and made their way to the stand to try and get out of being found guilty of murdering my son.

Directly along the wall opposite where we sat, was the Judge and her administrators. She sat up tall, a very petite older lady with a stern face. She wore glasses that I would often catch her peering over to look at those in the dock when they were acting up, laughing, or finding something that was given as evidence funny. The Judge was no nonsense and highly respected by those who worked in her presence. Something about her gave me confidence that she would see through the pretence that the defendants were displaying. I often wondered if she was a mother and how she felt about looking at me in the court room knowing that she was in charge of making the final decisions on what evidence could be heard, challenged, or held up, when others tried to challenge what was being presented. I wondered if she felt sympathy for what our family was going through. Every so often I would get a glimpse of emotion on her face, but she did an excellent job of keeping order in the court room, even when things went pear shaped.

Some of the defendant's family and friends were so difficult to manage. I had to stop any of my family and friends from going into the public gallery because of the way that they were intimidating them and causing conflicts. Andre's sister had spent days being interrogated in the public gallery and constantly had the defendants' families and friends making unnecessary comments towards her. This is why the decision to create a rota and add more chairs for my family and friends to attend and sit inside the court room came from. This was following an incident one day after court when I had a clash with one of the defendants' mothers. As we left the court after what had been a very stressful day listening to evidence, Andre's sister explained what torment that she had to listen to all day whilst she sat in the gallery by herself. I can't deny that I wasn't fed up because I was.

As we walked past the travel agents a few doors down from the Old Bailey I could see all the defendants' families and friends crammed inside collecting their belongings that they were not allowed to take into the courtroom. Admittedly I probably should have kept my cool, but I just couldn't. First their children had chased my son through the streets and hacked him to death without a care in the world. Then they are in the public gallery jeering and laughing with their children like it's the theatre and they're watching the story play out on the main stage. Blowing them kisses and attempting to throw them notes from the gallery and then to finish it off they were now intimidating and questioning the validity of Andre's sister being present in the gallery. It was her right to know what happened to her brother and I had a feeling take over me that I was no longer going to sit and be victim to their antics. I opened the door to the travel agents and as everyone stood with their backs to me, I made an announcement.

"This is Andre's sister, and she is allowed to be in the Public Gallery, so please leave her alone", I stated.

With that I turned around and walked away followed by my brother-in-law, Andre's sister and I thought, my younger sister. As I turned around, I could see Hayley holding onto the handle of the travel agent's door.

"What are you doing?", I asked her, slightly confused.

"She's coming", Hayley replied.

I could see the door opening and closing, opening, and closing as Hayley was trying to stop whoever was coming through the door from coming out.

"Let it go", I said, as we all stood there huddled together to see who was going to appear.

It was the driver's mother, who I didn't realise at first actually went to secondary school with me. If she hadn't kept making her comments, I never would have worked out who she was. It didn't matter anyway, there was no feeling there at all.

"Are you talking to me?", she shouted

"If you are the one that is intimidating Andre's sister, then yes", I responded.

She came right up to my face and started hurling abuse. I asked her to move away from me, as her saliva came flying out of her mouth hitting me in the face.

I put my hands up to try to stop her from coming any closer, but she continued to invade my personal space, until I pushed her away with my palms up against her shoulders. What came next, I totally did not expect.

"You know what you can do", she screamed, "rot in hell with your dead son!"

I stood with my mouth open as my blood started to bubble from deep down inside.

"At least I get to see my son again", she continued with the biggest smile across her face.

"I get to hug and kiss my boy; you can't do that cause yours is dead!" she shouted as she entered back inside the travel agents.

I was absolutely fuming, what a cold-hearted women and mother. All of that was not called for. I get the need to protect your children and have their backs even when they are in the wrong, sometimes, but your child is on trial for murder and at the moment there is no evidence to suggest that it was self-defence.

I couldn't help myself, I raged behind her and as she went inside, I grabbed her from behind. She turned around looking at me and with a big smile on her face she said, "Hit me Yemi, go on, I want you too".

I let go and left. I walked back to the Old Bailey and sobbed and sobbed uncontrollably. Despite the fact that she had no right to even talk about my son, she had got to me and that is what she wanted.
It wasn't until later that evening as I lay there in the bath, topped up to my neck with hot water with a brandy glass dangling over the edge, loosely held in my hand, that it dawned on me what she was trying to achieve. In the closing statements at the end of court, they always disclosed what evidence was coming up the next day. They had evidence regarding this mother, and she obviously didn't want me to hear it. As I lay there feeling defeated like I needed the day away from court, I quickly changed my mind and pulled myself together. I don't think that she wanted me to hear what was going to be said but I was sure that I wasn't going to miss a thing.

144

As predicted, the next day more evidence was shared by the Prosecuting team. They continued to deliver the forensic evidence that they had gathered and moved onto the clothing that was obtained from searches, belonging to the defendants. Each piece was photographed and placed in another evidence book that was being used in court as reference. As they referred to the range of items that they had retrieved and how it was relevant to the case I began to see the huge amount of work that was carried out in order to put this case together. The images of the clothing were linked to the CCTV footage that was seen of the defendants when they arrived at the scene. From this Police were then able to gather forensic evidence that linked them to each other and most importantly Andre.

There were trainers recovered that had Andre's blood on the sole of the feet and also another pair that had splatters on it. This would have only occurred by being in close contact with Andre when he was stabbed or when he was being kicked after he had been stabbed. There were also tracksuits that were drenched with blood, blood that was Andre's. I closed my eyes and took a deep breath as the realisation that the amount of blood loss that my son had contributed to his death. Then I turned to where the clothes were found, and this is when I realised the involvement of the driver's mother. There were Police officers who came to give evidence to the court as he had recovered several items linked to the case. The officer had been sat outside Mukasa's home address the morning after the murder when he witnessed the driver's mother leaving the address with a JD sports bag on her back. He thought it was suspicious so when she left in her car, they followed. On reaching her address she proceeded to enter her neighbour's house. Police approached the address and then took possession of the bag. Inside they found trainers and blood-stained clothes which later, after forensic examination, found had Andre's blood soaked into them. Was I shocked? Not really. I wouldn't put anything past her. She was desperate for her son not to be convicted. Out of all the families she was the one that caused the most contention throughout the trial. Her intimidation tactics, during lunchtimes and on the train on the journey home showed the type of character that she was.

What amazed me was that no charges came against her for trying to cover up and remove clothes that were evidence in a murder case. Seriously what was she going to do with them? Destroy them, wash them? Who knows I was just glad that Police were able to intercept and retrieve the items because they were key in proving involvement from the defendants? On cross examination it became apparent why charges were not brought against her.

"I gave her the wrong bag", said Mukasa.

"I was supposed to give her a bag of clothes for her son, things that didn't fit and I no longer wanted", he explained with his head held downwards.

I looked at him as he gave evidence. I couldn't help but to notice how small he was. He had a really small build, a bit like Andre but shorter. He had scruffy twists in his hair which the numerous witnesses referred to when they gave evidence. Every time they described who or what they saw, and it related to him, we knew. The hair was undeniable and joined with the yellow eyes presented to the jury here was Rodney otherwise known as Glare.

What was Glare accused of? Jumping out of the car, armed with a pole as seen on the CCTV. Hitting Andre across the face with the same said pole, carrying what many witnesses described as a handgun and having a Jamie Oliver knife set hidden in the garden of his home which matched one of the murder weapons. Not forgetting that the clothes that were retrieved matched those he was wearing as seen on the CCTV. These clothes were blood stained and matched Andre's blood. Things were not looking good for him as he sat on the stand being questioned by his barrister and cross examined by the prosecution. His own defence barrister was losing his temper with the level of lying that was going on. At one point the barrister closed his books and slammed them down on the bench as he publicly asked the entire court room what the point was of him putting a defence together and then made a dramatic exit from the court room.

Fabio or Femi as we now know he was called took the stand. The feeling that I had for him was different than the others.

I think that it was because I never had a relationship with any of them, but I did with him. I had warned Andre that he wasn't the type of friend that I wanted him to have and having taught him at school and having in my home meant that I knew what he was like. He couldn't deny that he was present on that day that my son lost his life, but he told so many lies to distance himself from the actual murder. There was so much evidence that came from his phone that showed his character and what he was capable of, which shocked me to see. There were two videos, one that showed Fabio playing with a shotgun and another one that showed him playing with knives and even going as far as threatening his girlfriend Charlie with them. When she gave evidence even though she was supposed to be a witness for the prosecution she tried really hard to try and portray Fabio as being someone who was kind and loving rather than the violent aggressor that we saw being played on our screens.

Fabio had also received a wound to his head and the explanation of how he received it was laughable.

"I was chasing Andre and we were running really fast when he just stopped and turned around holding a knife in the air. I tried to stop but the speed that I was going at made it difficult and as I turned, he stabbed me in the back of the head" he explained.

I sat shaking my head because as far as I was concerned, he was telling lies in order to try and make himself a victim instead of the real victim, Andre who was laying six feet in the ground. I was fuming. Did Andre stab him in the head? Probably. In self-defence, most definitely. Throughout the entire trial Fabio tried to present himself as being a victim and remove himself directly from the scene in any way he could. It was difficult at some points of the trial when hearing the evidence that the witnesses were giving to distinguish between Fabio and Ali because they had the same type of look.

"You must have really hated Andre", the prosecutor asked.

With full confidence and with a remorseful voice, that wasn't really remorse Fabio responded.

"No, actually he was a gentleman and I liked him".

This made me want to jump out of my seat and run across the short distance to where he was sitting and drag him down and inflict serious harm on him. In my mind all I could hope for was that every night when he closed his eyes or in his loneliest moments locked in his cell, all he would see was Andre's face and hear Andre's voice. Not on that day when he was murdered, but on the days when they were alright and hung out together having fun and getting up to mischief. He was the only one out of all the boys that had a friendship with Andre, and I wanted him to feel that friendship and the sound of Andre's laughter every minute of every day. I wanted it to haunt him like picturing my son laying dead in the mortuary or rotting in the ground was haunting me.

Fabio, I think probably had the best barrister. He was confident that he was going to get him off the charges and get him to walk free at the end. He was in a good position to argue the case because there was conflict between who did what and because Fabio was also injured an element of vulnerability. He started it. Without him this whole situation would not have happened. He was the link between Andre and his set of friends and Charlie who Andre had been defending because of the way that Fabio was treating her.

"He was in my business", Fabio told the court.

Yeah, he was, and I was proud of him for that. Charlie was Andre's friend and what Fabio had done to Charlie in front of Andre warranted someone stepping in. What kind of man would I have been raising if he had turned a blind eye and continued to be friends with someone, who was obviously growing into a women beater? I was proud of him for standing by her. It gave me a sense of pride about who my boy was and what he stood for. He would have been a good partner and father, that I was sure about, and these idiots had robbed him and me of the chance of ever seeing that happen. What made me even more angry was that Charlie was pregnant with Fabio's child. They were going to have the opportunity to be parents something that they had caused Andre to never be able to experience. It disgusted me. Their child was going to grow up knowing that both its parents contributed to someone else losing their life.

Charlie didn't want to see me. When she came to give evidence, she wanted to remain behind a curtain, and she also didn't want to bump into me anywhere in the building. This girl had been in my house practically every day, I treated her like a daughter. Even when Andre had got angry with her weeks prior to him being murdered for laughing at him for the criminal damage to my home and for continuing to contact Fabio and tell him where he was, I bloody defended her. Andre had taken her phone so that she couldn't keep calling Fabio on him and I went and got it back. He had no business taking the phone from her and when I drove to where he was to challenge him, he handed it over straight away without question. I understood why he had done it, but it was wrong, and I would always try to get Andre to do the right things in life.

Her evidence was flimsy. She was supposed to be on the prosecutions side but couldn't help but defend the man that she clearly had feelings for. I didn't really expect anything different from her. Did I blame her? Partially but not entirely. She was young and in love. Pregnant and emotional. Trying to do the right thing but yet it was still coming out wrong. I really wish that I had been given the chance to speak to her. I think I would have hugged her and set her mind at ease. Maybe that makes me soft, but I know that she loved Andre too. She was in a conflicting situation, and I believe that she was scared of Fabio. After all he had beat her up, locked her in the boot of the car and put a knife to her even if it was, in his eyes, in jest. I would have been scared of him too if I was her age. I just pray that for the future, having a child, she makes better life choices to keep herself and her child safe.

Seeing Ali take the stand made my blood boil even more. Straight faced wearing a pullover jumper and glasses. A disguise to make himself look intelligent. It was a shame that he wasn't really intelligent. The evidence that was given showed him to be the dumbest criminal ever and at one stage prior to arrest he must have really thought that he was going to get away with it. There was something about this boy that gave me a chill down my spine. He was cold. Throughout his evidence he remained straight faced with no emotion. There were a few days throughout the trial where he just refused to come to court.

The witness statements and the CCTV that was presented made it undeniable that he was involved. He was the one that apparently inflicted the most injuries on my son's tiny body. The black blade and handled knife that was recovered shortly after also matched the set that was found in his mother's kitchen drawer. It matched the Snap Chat video that he posted waving it around and threatening Andre and his friends that he was going to shank them!

Ali's clothes had also been retrieved; he was wearing them at the time he was arrested. The same clothes that he was seen wearing on CCTV when he jumped out of the car waving the same knife in the air and then later the following day on the CCTV at The Goat Pub on the Shrublands Estate. There was lots of forensic evidence which tied Ali to Andre's murder, and he knew it. You could see on his face that he knew that he had gone too far. His friends who he was out running with were now selling him down the river in order to try and secure their own freedom. The evidence that annoyed me more than any of the evidence about what happened on that day was the revelation that there had been a number of incidents prior to August 16th which could have stopped the murder of my son had they have been dealt with swiftly.

A Police officer who was giving evidence revealed that Ali had been in contact with Police in the weeks leading up to Andre's murder. Not only was he on Police tag he was also stopped on a few occasions, three in fact. The Police stated that late one evening they had been notified that a car had crashed into several cars and the passage was now slumped in the driver seat of his car. When Police attended, they found Ali in an intoxicated state. He had been driving and crashed into several parked vehicles before parking up on the side of the road. In the boot of the car was part of the shotgun. This must have been the same one that was used to shoot Alex in the face. There was also blank credit cards and live ammunition. Like seriously, I couldn't understand how he had been caught with a gun and not been detained. I was furious. The officer explained that the gun was incomplete, if the butt was missing from the gun, then it was legal to carry. They also revealed that he had stopped on two separate occasions in the possession of samurai swords. Ali didn't care, he knew this was the case and sat there calmly.

The other incidents were car related. Cars were chased from Monks Hill after several complaints from members of the public were called into Police. They were chased and then the cars abandoned, and the passengers decamped through the woodlands. Inside the car were knives. On the night that Andre was killed it was revealed that Police had visited the home of Fabio to speak to his brother about the car that was abandoned and confiscated. Fabio was pretending to be his brother when talking to Police, they knew this, and when Police left, they watched as the boys left the house and got into the car before travelling directly to the scene and killing Andre. Maybe, just maybe if Police had taken their chances that night and pulled even one in for questioning, my son would still be alive now. I sat there trying to digest all of the information that I had heard. Sometimes it felt as though I was trapped inside a glass dome watching and hearing everything that was going on in the court room as if I wasn't really there. My mind was unable to process quick enough all the information that I had to listen to. It made no sense to me. If I could go back in time and change just one thing it could have made a difference.

I couldn't bear to look at him. Being in the same space, breathing the same air, listening to the same information made me uncomfortable. Out of all the witnesses so far, Ali just came across as cold hearted, affected by life itself. I couldn't put my finger on it. To come so up close and personal with someone and then carry out such a vicious unprovoked attack on someone that you barely know has to make you a special kind of crazy. I wondered what kind of traumas he had experienced in his own life and why he didn't value someone else's life and clearly his own. He also had a child, one that he was fighting to be a father of against struggles and discrimination. Hearing that Ali had a child of his own made me question even more what was actually going through his head. When you bring a life into the world you know how precious that life is. To be a parent should give you the understanding of what life means and how bringing someone else into the world gives you not only a lifelong responsibility but an unconditional love. Why would he take that away from me?

The final defendant to take the stand was Jamell. Out of all four of the defendants he was the one that I cared least about. I guess from the evidence that I had already heard from the other prosecutors it appeared that he had the least involvement in the entire attack. Jamell had been arrested in the early hours of the morning after Andre had been pronounced dead. He lied from the beginning. He had concocted a story that he had been called to the scene by his friend who had suffered a head injury. He distanced himself from Rodney and Ali by even suggesting that the people that were chasing Andre on the night were unknown to him. Just people who lived on the estate. Complete and utter denial at his interviews about knowing anything to do with Andre's murder or any conflicts that had been going on between the two groups. As the interview played out in court, I watched him closely. He was tall, taller than the others and slim and he looked vulnerable. Not like the others who showed little remorse. He often sat looking down at the floor, never tried to have eye contact with me as the evidence about the part that he played was unveiled he looked more and more regretful and embarrassed that he had been caught in a lie.

There was no sympathy from me. At no time did I feel sorry for him finding himself in this situation. The prosecution at the start of the trial outlined everyone's involvement and made it clear that everyone involved played their part in making sure that Andre was murdered on that night. A tactical team. All working together to carry out a task. A task that they completed successfully. Jamell was the driver. He drove all of the defendants to the scene. He stopped so they could jump out, he followed the chase and then once the deed was committed, he drove them all home making sure that they were well away from the scene. His DNA from the sock that was covered around the handle of the knife was recovered and also trainers were found in the compost heap of his home address they were ceased and checked for DNA. The forensic team revealed that there was contact blood staining found on the toe of the trainers that matched Andre's DNA and indicated that he had been in direct contact with Andre at some stage during the attack. Jamell couldn't deny that he was there.

The level of involvement that he had was unclear before now and as I looked at him sat there in the stand; I could feel some resemblance to Andre. In terms of the positions that they played in their friendship groups I think that Andre and Jamell were very similar. Andre was athletic, he played football, finished school with his GCSE's, loved his family, had ambition, and generally got dragged along by his friendships. Jamell sounded the same. How I wish that he had been strong enough to just say no. To take the control away from his friends who had dragged him along on that day. He may not have inflicted any injuries using knives, but he played a major part in the way that the day played out. If he hadn't have driven them there, they wouldn't have been able to reach the estate as quickly as they had. Maybe that would have given Andre longer to evaluate the situation when his so-called friends didn't arrive and leave. The fact that he then drove them all home after they committed the level of injuries that they did and along the way watched as they threw the murder weapons out of the windows meant that he understood fully what had just been carried out. The sheer fact that he tried to get rid of any clothing and footwear that he was wearing at the time and then lied during his interviews meant that he was trying to cover up everything that happened, and he was doing that for himself and his friends. I could not help but think that this made him just as guilty and for that he was just as bad as the others who actually carried out the stabbings. I could only but pray that he too would be held accountable for the part that he played.

The evidence books that were used inside the courtroom were large and contained so much evidence. The book that obsessed me the most was the one that had pages and pages of phone data in date order from the calls and cell sites of the defendants, Andre and his friends and a few other individuals who had spent time with either of them at times. I was amazed by the level of detail that the phone data revealed but horrified at what the data appeared to show. The morning of Andre's murder the cell data showed that the four defendants and Andre's friends were all in the same vicinity and their phones were all picking up signal from the same cell tower.

"Can you explain why all your phones were in the same place", the barrister asked.

"Because we met up to squash the argument", Fabio explained.

They had all met up, but I knew that Andre was not aware of this. Did his own friends decide to set him up so that they could get out of the conflicts? The information only got worse. The phone that Katy had asked me about previously was the phone that was calling Andre on the drive down and then seconds later calling Ali. This happened a few times. The data also showed that the two groups of friends had been talking to each other on various days on the lead up to the murder and also that after they had jumped in the car and headed off the estate the first person that was called was Andre's friend Brandon, the one who Andre was supposed to be meeting on that senseless day.

No charges came to any of those boys, and this really bothered me for a long time. Nothing could be proved. The barrister explained that without actual proof of what was being said in the conversations the data alone could not prove a set up. They could have been talking about the football scores. They weren't though, because every single defendant, in their time on the stand stated that they knew that Andre was there because his own friends told them. Were they telling the truth? What would be their reasons for lying?

CHAPTER SIXTEEN
THE TRIAL VERDICTS AND SENTENCING

It was over. Everything that I could hear, see, or know had been shared and it was now in the hands of the selected Jury to decide what the outcomes were going to be. I was exhausted, I had an overwhelming amount of information and images lodged inside my brain that I couldn't get rid of. It was as if it was swirling around inside my memory and parts of the information that I had been listening for the last twelve weeks were presenting themselves to me at the most inconvenient moments of the day and holding me hostage to the thoughts that were playing out.

After the Jury retired to deliberate and make their final decisions about who did what and whether or not they were actually guilty of murder, or whether they should be freed back out into society to get on with their live, the waiting continued. I had been in court for almost twelve weeks. I had spent Andre's birthday inside that court room and my birthday was looming. Every day I attended the court, signed in, and then hung about waiting for the call to say that the Jury had reached their verdicts. I was shown to a small waiting room inside Victim Services, it looked like a small living room with comfortable chairs and a small television on a highly polished wooden sideboard. The décor was in keeping with the rest of the court building's interior. Expensive, well-kept but old fashioned. I spent days sat there watching their carefully selected set of DVDs. This was the first time that I watched the film 'Shirley Valentine. Mandy raved about the film, but I had never watched it and honestly never even heard of it. We laid there watching DVDs, but I couldn't relax. Every time my phone sent a notification or rang my heart would jump out of my chest. I was a nervous wreck; I played the evidence over and over in my head. After a few days I could sense that the verdict was coming soon. I prepared my family to make sure that they were all there and able to be present when the verdict came in. The phone rang, it was Katy.

"Hi Yemi, are you near?" she asked in a calm voice.

Katy always had a calm voice, no matter what was happening her professionalism allowed her to keep control and keep us all calm.

"The Jury have reached a verdict and the court will resume in thirty minutes", she told me.

My heart was racing. I made all the necessary phone calls to the family members that I needed to be there to check where they were and then once they arrived, we all made our way into the courtroom via the security desk. The security team had got to know us. They must have known that I was the mother of a murder victim, they had seen me attend court every day for the last three months, sometimes in the worst state, a nervous wreck or a face drained of all emotion, but today was going to bring that daily routine to an end. We made our way up the large staircase which stood proud in the middle of the grand foyer and up to court room 8. Outside was a crowd of people. Everyone that had been to the case had come to hear what the outcome was going to be. The prosecutors approached; they didn't look concerned, so I was going to take this a positive. I mean no one really knew what the outcome was going to be, but they had done this process so many times I think they were able to gauge outcomes based on the level of evidence that was given and also the length of time that the Jury take to deliberate.

I felt nervous, my stomach was in knots. The decisions made by the Jury today would prove that those four sat in the dock really were responsible for taking my sons life. I knew that they were anyway, but I needed someone to actually tell me that on a factual level. Everyone entered the court room. The defendant's inside the dock, the press, the judge and then the jury. The court clerk instructed the jury foreman to stand.

"In the case of Femi Cela, have you all reached a verdict upon which are all agreed?" she asked.

"Yes", the foreman responded.

Did I really want to hear the outcome? I couldn't look. I could feel my eyes filling up and I felt as if I was holding my breath.

"For the charge of murder for Femi Cela, do you find the defendant guilty or not guilty", she asked.

I held my breath and the tears. Then after what felt like an eternity the outcome came.

"Not Guilty"

I exhaled as the entire public gallery erupted. I couldn't look up. What did I just hear? Can this be right, really!

I turned my head to the left to see Fabio sat there in the dock with a grin on his face smiling up at his family in the gallery above. The Judge banged her gabble down on the table to regain silence. There was a celebration happening in the gallery above that eventually simmered back down to a silent whisper. As I glimpsed him, I could see that he was still smiling, got away with murder, I felt as if I could physically vomit. My sister took my hand, we couldn't believe the outcome that had been shared. The clerk continued.

"For the lesser charge of manslaughter for Femi Cela, do you find the defendant guilty or not guilty", she asked.

"Guilty", the foreman replied.

There was an airy silence. No more celebrating from the dock or the gallery. From the previous outburst of celebratory noise to a sudden silent hum moving throughout the courtroom. I couldn't help but to let out a cry which I quickly sucked back in. I had become used to hiding my emotions. From the defendants, my family, my children, and my friends. I had created a coping mechanism in my head that enabled me to instantly stop myself from crying publicly. It was quite simple. I would talk to myself. I would allow my inner voice to tell me off and demand that I take back control.

"Stop it Yemi, stop it Yemi, stop it Yemi", my inner voice would demand.

I know that this sounds like a very weird coping strategy, but it worked for me.

Although on reflection it probably wasn't a very healthy way to deal with the grief and overwhelming emotion that I was feeling during different situations throughout the trial or in general day to day life, but it worked for me. It helped me to maintain my dignity and to keep composed and in turn I was able to listen, understand and make informed decisions about things that I needed to see happening or how I reacted to the information I was told. I couldn't help but to look at Fabio again. He had now turned from smiling and looking up at his family to sitting with his head in his hands. I wondered what he was thinking. He went from thinking that he was going to be freed to now knowing that he was definitely going to prison.

Next was the verdict for Ali, surely this could not be manslaughter too. I looked at him as he looked straight out of the dock. Dressed smartly in a shirt with a pullover, neatly trimmed hair and wearing reading glasses. Nothing like the photos that had been posted in the newspapers of him or those that had been floating around social media. The verdicts continued.

"For the charge of murder for Ali Zahawy, do you find the defendant guilty or not guilty", the clerk asked.

I looked up willing the foreman to release the verdict that I was hoping for. I did not want this young man out on the street. From all the evidence that had been given throughout the trial there could only be one possible outcome.

"Guilty", he responded.

Again, I fought back the tears. These were not tears of joy but tears of relief. Finally, the truth was known. These people were guilty of murdering my son and this was no longer questionable. There was no noise. The gallery remained quiet apart from one female voice that you could hear making crying noises. I presumed that it was Ali's mother. I think any mother would have been overwhelmed hearing everything that your child was capable of doing and then finding that the jury was unanimous in their decision that he had taken the life of someone else's child. He was guilty, he didn't move. He didn't show one bit of emotion. Not like Fabio. He just sat there facing the front in exactly the same way that he had done throughout the entire trial. Why was he so emotionless? Surely, he couldn't just not care about what he had done. As I looked at him, I thought that maybe he had been prepared for this outcome during his time on remand. Maybe this entire trial was just being played out in the courtroom, but he already knew what his chances looked like and that it wasn't going to be one where he was going to walk out a free man.

That was two down. I was halfway through the verdicts, and I already felt as if I had heard enough for one day. I knew that this needed to be over and done with and I wanted it to happen quickly. By now I was fidgeting. The anxiety of all the highs and lows was tormenting me, and this was playing out in the form of rocking and trembling of my legs. I kept my composure. Rodney's verdict was up next.

I wasn't sure about Rodney, not one hundred percent like I had been for Ali. The evidence weighed heavily on him, there was so much to suggest that he contributed to the death of my son. Although saying this, he was the one that probably did the most during the trial to try and convince the jury that he was innocent. His barrister had given up all hope for him because of the amount of lies that he had told throughout. Not only was Rodney linked to a knife, but witnesses had also described seeing him with a pole and a gun. The barrister had spent an incredible amount of time trying to convince the jury that Rodney was not in possession of a gun but did have a knife for him to only then himself try to convince the jury that it was a BB gun that didn't work. That gun, whatever it was never was recovered so I will never know what it was but can only imagine the terrifying moment that he had held it to my son's head during the horrific attack.

"For the charge of murder for Rodney Mukasa, do you find the defendant guilty or not guilty", she asked.

"Guilty", he told the courtroom.

Again, another unanimous decision. The relief came over me. All those that I believed in my heart of hearts put a hand on my son were going to face prison time for what they had done.

There was only one left to go, and this was Jamell Lonergan. Consistently the evidence showed that Jamell had been at the scene and despite the fact that his mother and I had caught up early on in the trial I didn't want to see anyone be convicted or go to prison for longer than they should. I was surprised that I felt this way, after all, each of their individual actions contributed to my boy being murdered and me having to live out these past few months in hell. I still wanted it to be fair. Ali and Rodney were found guilty and for me that was fair and justified. With Fabio's verdict I was not so convinced that he should have got manslaughter and now it was to see what Jamell's fate would be.

The foreman delivered the news that the jury had not been able to reach a unanimous decision and therefore a verdict had not yet been reached. I wasn't surprised. I think even if I was on the jury, I would have had to have questioned and re questioned his involvement to make sure that the right decision was made. Nothing more could be added about his verdict today. I looked at the prosecuting barrister who gave me the nod to let me know that he would discuss this with me after the proceedings.

That was it. I looked over at the dock where all four defendants sat. One guilty of manslaughter and the other two most definitely guilty of my son's murder. Jamell and Fabio were the closest by far. They had talked about their friendship since nursey school during the trial. I think it was this loyalty to Fabio that encouraged Jamell to follow along with their foolishness. I could tell from the evidence that he was giving that he wasn't a bad person, I think that friendships can sometimes do this to you. They both sat there in tears. Fabio and Jamell were both sat in the dock looking at each other crying. Apart from the obvious reasons for crying at that particular time, I wondered what they were thinking. Was Jamell upset for his friend receiving a guilty verdict for manslaughter. Did he worry about how he would cope? Was Fabio wallowing in his own self-pity or worried about the fact that Jamell hadn't yet received a verdict? Whatever was going on for them two in the dock made them stand out like sore thumbs. As they continued to cry, I began to notice a tension in the dock from what appeared to be between Rodney and Ali.

Rodney had been sitting there in the dock after receiving his verdict as if he had been zapped by a taser. He was almost lifeless with no reaction until now. He must have been pondering over what had been said in his own head and it had now hit him like a lightning bolt. You could see that he was becoming restless, moving around in his seat and I could hear him repeating the words "I need to get out".

After a short while, Rodney stood up in the dock and with some haste to his walk he headed towards the door that led to the holding cells at the back of the court room. As he passed Ali who continued to sit in the same seat, still without movement or emotion I could hear Rodney yelling.

"Fucking murderer, fucking prick"

Within another split second the dock exploded with an uproar as Ali jumped out of his seat and lunged at Rodney. There was a scuffle. Everyone in the courtroom and public gallery was on their feet. It was strange how friendships could turn so sour so quickly. Throughout the trial it was clear to see that there were divides forming between the four defendants who were once such close friends that they confided in each other enough to commit murder. There was absolutely no control over anything that was happening inside or outside of the dock. As I sat frozen in my seat five out of the ten security officers that were inside the dock with the defendants moved toward Ali and restrained him. Both Ali and Rodney were eventually taken out of the courtroom and as the courtroom went back to silence you could still hear them in the background shouting and kicking off with one another.

The other two who remained in the dock were visibly upset by what had happened between their friends. Fabio was on his feet pacing up and down as the security officers gained control of the situation. He was liked a scared caged animal looking up at his family for help. There was no helping him now. The decisions had been made and it was only going to be the length of sentence that could give him some hope and clarity about what his future was going to look like. Jamell was still sat with his head in his hands, crying. The security officers then approached Fabio, it was his time to leave and go back down to the cells. As he did so, he shock Jamell's hand and patted him on the back before making his way through the doors that his fighting friends had passed through shortly before.

That was it. The courtroom went back to being under control, the judge addressed Jamell that there would be a retrial as no decision was going to be made and set a time for sentencing tomorrow morning. The gallery was cleared, and my friends and family were escorted back to the Victim Services area where we had spent so much time waiting for the verdicts to come in. So much was happening, the verdicts had been reported on live as they were happening and so many people from the local community were responding on social media about the outcomes. There was an element of relief in the air that the truth had been told and now all we could do was wait for the sentencing the next day. We hung around to give the other families the chance to clear the pavements outside and make their way home on the trains that we normally shared together on our journeys to and from The Old Bailey. Emotions were most definitely going to be high, and I was too exhausted for any conflicts to occur again today. I spoke to the prosecution before I left the building to get an update on what the next steps were going to be for Jamell. The prosecutors were going to try and make a deal with Jamell's barristers because having an entire new trial would have been timely and costly to everyone involved. I for one did not want to have to go back to the court for a retrial. It was suggested that Jamell would probably plead guilty to the lesser charge of manslaughter and accept a sentence in the same day for the part he played.

In my heart I was happy with that. This needed to be over with and although there was evidence to suggest that he had got out of the car and some stage of the attack it was unknown from the evidence if he contributed to any of the injuries that Andre sustained. Having all four convicted and sentenced for their parts that they played gave me some peace of mind. The evening was long. As usual when there had been some level of disclosure around the case, social media went mad. I was receiving so many messages not only from people who I knew on Facebook but also reporters and unknown individuals who had followed the entire trial. Tomorrow was going to be another hard day when the number of years that each of the defendant's needed to serve was revealed but then that chapter would be over.

Everyone came over to the house. It almost seemed like a celebratory event but for me it wasn't. As the evening drew to a close, I gathered up some overnight belongings and went to stay with the man who made me feel safe. I spent the night mostly awake. I cried, I imagined what tomorrow would bring but most of all I felt some comfort knowing that they were not coming back out for what I was hoping would be a long while.

The next morning, I made my way to the Old Bailey. There were so many people turning up today to witness what would be the last day of this trial. My family and friends were coming into the courtroom in order to keep us all separated. Some arrived in T-shirts with Andre's face on them, but the court rules meant that they needed to remove them. There was a buzz outside the Old Bailey with so many people queuing to get into the public gallery to see the final outcome. Was this going to be the justice that was needed?

As the proceedings began an announcement was made to the court about the behaviour that was expected in the courtroom for everyone that had decided to come today for the proceedings. There had been so much trouble and inappropriate behaviour, including the defendants making gun gestures with their hands to members of my family sat in the gallery that the court were taking no chances on what was going to be a high-tension day. We sat waiting patiently. I had made the decision to allow Ashley to come to the court today. He was now fifteen years old and although I could have let him come on some of the previous trial dates, I didn't think that it was appropriate to traumatise him with all the evidence that was being disclosed about what happened to his brother. Today however was a historic day that I wanted him to be part of. He sat next to me silently looking in the dock at the boys that were now convicted of killing his brother. He knew them all. Not only had they attended the school that he went too, but he had also often hung out with Andre and Fabio when they had been friends. Ashley also had a brother on his dad's side of the family, and they had been friends prior to the murder of Andre.

On closer inspection of the dock, I noticed that there were only three sat inside. Ali hadn't come for his sentencing instead he wrote a note to the judge excusing himself and giving his reasons which basically, just sounded like an "I don't care" type of note. Fabio was the first to be sentenced He sat there silently as the Judge read out her findings from the trial. She was clear about the fact that Fabio was the one who orchestrated the mob-handed attack and for this reason she was handing him a sixteen-year sentence with an extended licence. I didn't understand what this meant but knew that she was serious about the role that Fabio had played and made it clear that if it wasn't for him than this terrible tragedy would probably not have happened. As the proceedings continued, the judge handed life sentences to both Rodney and Ali in his absence. Twenty-two years each before applying for parole. The Judge and clerks did a lot of back and forth with numbers as the barristers put in their mitigating circumstances including taking into consideration the ages of the defendants when the crime was committed. There was a lot of legal jargon which I didn't really understand but I just watched as the conversations went across the courtroom from all those who wore black cloaks and white curly wigs. It was over, not only was I extremely emotional but also exhausted from it all. I had spent so long travelling to and from the court in the last three months and listening to the overwhelming information about what actually happened to my son on that sunny evening in August, today it had come to an end.

We got up and returned to the victim's services area to have final deliberations and have all the finer details explained to us. Did I really listen or take it all in? No, of course I didn't. My brain was not in a position to absorb any more information. I was told that the press had setup outside of the courtroom and were expecting a statement and interview from me. I didn't mind talking to the press, I thought that it was important for communities to know what we were going through as a family in the hope that they might pick up any signs that their own children were in situations similar and prevent the murder of their loved ones. I also wanted the community to know that I was thankful for all the support that they had offered to us all. That was important for me. I had been transparent from the beginning and although I didn't ask for or look for stories to be written or to even be included in youth violence related events it seemed to be all I ever got invited to anymore.

As I looked at myself in the bathroom mirror, splashed water on my face I could see the wear and tear that this trial had had on me. Loosing Andre and then having to relive every step of his murder at such a public event had taken its toll on me. I had lost so much body weight and I just about recognised myself. I had to pull myself together for one last time and make my way outside to the pavement where the press was waiting. Following police with my own family following me, I was escorted down to the front doors of the Old Bailey. This would be the last time that I would stand in this foyer and pass the security. I thanked them for their support, their smiles, their understanding every morning and made my way outside.

Flashing lights, microphones and a sea of people awaited me. It took my breath away. As I stepped out on the pavement with police in front of me, I watched as an official statement was given. Once the inspector had finished speaking, she turned to look at me.

"Is it me now?", I asked.

With a gentle smile on her face, she nodded at me to go ahead and speak. I didn't know what I was going to say. I never planned anything and inside I was scared. My stomach didn't feel good, my throat felt dry, and I was battling emotionally inside to hold in the tears.

"I would like to say that I am pleased with the sentences that have been handed out today to the young men who were involved in the murder of my son", I said as I sucked the tears back up.

"For me this is the start of the next step because no matter how many years they serve, it is not going to return my son back to me. So today I am going to draw a line and try to move on to having a better life for my two remaining children and to ask that all the young people out there who are tearing families apart, to stop doing what they are doing and start thinking about the consequences of their actions, to stop the violence towards each other. There are four families today that have lost their children, there are other ways to deal with the issues that they have"

From there I moved on to speak to ITV news, still trying to hold everything together and make my boy proud. All I wanted to do was go home to my boys and hug them and make sure that they understood that these boys that had ruined our lives were now going to spend a long time behind bars unable to hurt any of us anymore.

CHAPTER SEVENTEEN
THE DAYS AFTER

There were several related things that happened once the trial was over. Just when I thought that fight was over, I had to start a completely new set of struggles. I was still living in temporary accommodation directly opposite the place that my son was murdered, and it was having a huge effect on my everyday life. Some nights as I would drive home, instead of taking the left turning home I would turn right and end up sitting on the wall where Andre was laying on the grass bleeding to death. I had an urge to lay on the grass to feel close to him. I rubbed my hands on the grass to feel what he felt beneath him on that night as the emotion rose once more up my chest, into my throat and out of my eyes as tears. This really wasn't a healthy way to live. If the cemetery was open throughout the night, I probably would have found myself there again night after night. This needed to change. Continuing to return to this area was not good for my mental health. As silly as it may sound, I was scared for the boys being here. I didn't know who else played what part in my son's death, especially after the phone data evidence, and we were too close to Monk's Hill for comfort. I needed to make moving a priority.

Apart from Andre telling me catastrophically not to return to my husband before he died, he also told me not to give up on the council. He had watched me for years struggling to pay the rent from the private sector and he also knew how important it was for me to have a stable home. I had left home at the age of fifteen and moved around with my belongings in a bag. I needed a stable home for the boys. Somewhere where they could feel safe and secure, somewhere they could call home and somewhere that didn't give them the constant reminder of the greatest thing that we had lost in our lives. It took me just over three months to secure a home for me and my boys. I honestly didn't think that it was going to be so difficult to do but I persevered and sent emails on top of emails to every single department and person that I thought would be able to help. I started bidding on all types of different properties in all different areas in the hope that I would see that number go to one to say that I was the most eligible. It became like a full-time job. It was frustrating and I had to keep on top of all the different conversations that I was making but finally on one July morning I received the phone call that I had been hoping for. The council had found me a two-bedroom home in Addiscombe. I had to go and collect the keys and sign the paperwork.

I felt bad about the situation, I had grown up being a very independent person, making my way in life and finding a way to always provide for my own children but I was weak, and I didn't have the funds to get a deposit together and seek accommodation on my own without support. I was due to go back to work in September and was desperate to get settled before then. There was no viewing beforehand, whatever I was offered I was grateful to receive. I left the council office and made my way to the property. As we drove, I prayed that the house had no resemblance to the house that we had lived in on Monks Hill. I really didn't want a house with same layout only because the boys found it extremely difficult to accept a bedroom that they always felt belonged to their brother. I would have loved a three-bedroomed house as both boys had adopted their own coping strategies from the grief that they were going through.
One slept with the door firmly shut with the lights off whilst the other needed lights on and someone sleeping next to him. As we pulled up to the house it was hard to tell from the outside what the inside was going to be like. Nervously I approached the front door and turned the key. It didn't really matter what it was like I was going to make it home and start picking up some of the pieces of our shattered lives. Inside there was a small hallway with two doors one on the left and one directly opposite on the right. The stairs run up the middle of the hall between the two doors. As I opened the doors, I could see a long kitchen on one side and a living room on the other.

The house was definitely different. The kitchen had a strange layout. There were a set of patio doors at one end that led out to a small, pebbled garden at the front of the house. At the other end of the kitchen was a normal kitchen door. When I opened it, it led out to a concrete garden fenced off with a back gate. Neither of the gardens touched each other they were totally separate. I wondered what else this strange little house entailed. We headed up stairs to a small landing with five doors. I opened one door to a double sized bedroom and then made my way around the landing in a clockwise motion. Next to that bedroom was a bathroom, then an airing cupboard.

The next door that I opened led to another double sized bedroom with a built-in wardrobe and that left only one other door. Another storage cupboard perhaps? As I pushed the door open there was a wall in front of me but as I continued inside, I suddenly realised that it was a very small double bedroom. The master bedroom had been properly partitioned into two bedrooms. I couldn't believe my luck; I must have a guardian angel looking out for me. I smiled and instantly felt at home.

It wasn't easy. We moved in very quickly with hardly anything. The boys never had any beds or bedroom furniture. We had a sofa and a few odd pieces of furniture that we had put into storage in a hurry before we went to Kent, our clothes and that was about it. I didn't own a fridge cooker, washing machine or anything that I had prior. I really did need to start from scratch, but it was okay. I had a good feeling about the fresh start and even without anything I was determined to make this home and that was exactly what I did. For about two weeks we camped out in the front room. We used the mattress from the bed that I had laid out on the floor to snuggle up with each other. During the days I spent my time painting over the red and blue ceilings that the previous owner felt were acceptable colours for ceilings. Slowly, with the help from family and friends I managed to carpet the boys' bedrooms and purchase them beds and blinds and minimal bedroom furniture. We had lost so much but now it was time to build ourselves back up and, on a wish, and a prayer we got there.

I did manage to fulfil my wish to take my children away for a much-needed getaway. My mum paid for us to all go to Turkey for a week. I had not been on holiday with my mum since the holiday to Greece with Andre when he was still young. She needed that break with us as much as we needed it. Amari was like a different child abroad. He laughed, he played with other children, and he felt confident. It was amazing to see them enjoying themselves. I relaxed by the pool, the heat was scorching, and I finally felt at peace. Being so far away from home did something for me. The escape to Jamaica and now

Turkey was doing me the world of good. The only thing that I could not escape was the publicity around my son's death. So many people had seen the media attention around Andre's murder and seen me in newspapers and through television coverage. I couldn't escape it. All the way in Turkey and people knew what we had been through.

The same thing happened in Jamaica when I visited the beautiful Island for a second time that same year. I was lucky enough to have a niece who worked for Virgin and anytime she could offer low price fares, Mandy and I would board the plane. People knew me all around the world. I was pleased for Andre's name being on the tip of everyone's tongues as for me it meant that he wasn't being forgotten but sometimes I just wanted to be left alone. I wanted the boys to have fun without people constantly reminding us of the traumas that we had been through. We knew the trauma, we were living with the pain every single day, there was nothing that we could do to escape it. One minute we would be laughing and having fun and then we would catch ourselves in a happy moment and feel guilty for having fun when Andre was no longer with us.

It didn't take me long to get the house into a liveable state and to get the boys moods up to feel some sort of normality. Normal would never be the same again but we, the three of us, had to try to live again and shift our grief to a place that was manageable on a day-to-day basis. My main priority was to be able to return to work in September. It was important for me to not lose the independence that I had built for myself and the staff team that I had at work were just the right people that I would need to support me on my return. I was scared but keen to get back. Not only because I was becoming comfortable with being at home, pottering around all day long and spending time with my family but also because the school that I taught in was also the school that Andre had attended for five years. There were so many happy memories in that school that I felt a comfort when I walked inside the door. Andre being marched towards my classroom to leave those coats that I now think of so fondly. Watching him play football as part of the school team on the green fields that surrounded our concrete jungle. Picturing him and his friends sat in the corridors during breaks and lunches and seeing that immense pride that he had on his face when he told people that I was his mum. I wasn't always a teacher, Andre witnessed that happen. The two younger boys didn't know anything different, but he did, and he respected me for the hard work that I put in to get there.

One day as I sat in the garden soaking up the sunshine, I received a phone call from my family liaison officer. During the investigation and the trial, it became a really common theme to receive calls from her on a really regular basis, but now that it was all over, every time her name flashed up on my screen, I went into panic mode before answering.

"Hi Yemi, how are you?" Katy asked.

I did not anticipate what she was about to tell me. As usual she was always the one that had to give me good news and updates, but it was also her job to break the bad news too. During the investigation and the trial, she had become that go to person for any type of questions that we had. I do not envy her with the job that she does, but I think that we made this job for her easier. Easier in the sense that we were so open and honest as a family. We allowed her to gain a real insight into the dynamics of our family and we also were not very needy. Mandy is definitely a 'get things done' kind of women and I think that her influence over me, during all the years that I had known her had well and truly rubbed off.

"Two of the boys convicted have appealed their sentences", she told me.

I don't think that I was really surprised at all to be honest. I wouldn't put anything past them. They didn't accept what they had done during the trial so why would they accept it now.

"It is common" she continued.

This just made me angry. Surly the first stages of rehabilitation would be acceptance. So here we were now looking at going back to the court of appeal for Fabio and Rodney because they were not happy. Seriously, who did they think they were? Twenty-two years for murder and sixteen years for manslaughter and you want to argue the toss for less time. Did they think that they were having too much of their lives taken away. What about the life that they took away from my son? The appeals were in and there was nothing that I could do about it but go along with the process and again turn up at court to hear the outcome. This didn't happen straightaway; it took a while before it was brought to court again but on the day in question, I attended again to hear the verdicts.

Both boys attended via video link on screens that were on the wall of the large courtroom situated behind where I was sat. Throughout the proceedings I had the urge to turn around and look at them. I was curious as to how prison life was treating them and if they still felt as smug as they did throughout the trial. I didn't look. Although the temptation was there, I kept my head turned to the front. I no longer had any time for them, the last think I was going to give them was my emotion. Fabio was represented by the same barrister that he had for the trial. This man was intent on getting his client off the hook. Appeals are not paid for by legal aid so maybe he was just happy that Fabio's family had the money to pay him for his leg work and then the day in court putting the case forward for consideration. Rodney on the other hand, did not have a barrister present. Instead, his case was being conducted by his mother. I wondered whether this was because they couldn't find anyone who was willing enough to try to get him off a murder conviction. It probably wasn't that it was probably the lack of available funds that his family had to pay for a barrister to represent him.

The proceedings began but for the most part of the hearing I didn't have a clue what they were all going on about. Katy would occasionally lean across and make gestures that what had just been said was good and in our favour and that was really about all I knew. The gist of the reasons for appeal from what I understood was that Fabio felt that he should have had a sentence that was more in line with his friend Jamell. He felt as though his input was just about the same as his driver friend even though the evidence showed that he played a much larger role in the entire tragedy. He wanted to have his sentence reduced to ten years so that he could serve five and be release back out into society. Currently his sixteen-year sentence should have meant that he served eight years behind bars and then been released with the remaining eight years being served on licence. The judge made a point of giving Fabio an extended licence meaning that he had to serve a minimum of two thirds of his sentence behind bars, almost eleven years, before being considered for parole. From this he was also given a four-year extended licence so would remain under supervision until he reached a total of twenty years. I think he really should have been convicted for murder with the others, but this was the judge's way at the time of making sure that he got as close to the twenty-two years that the others received.

Rodney's appeal was mainly based on the fact that he didn't have a good relationship with his barrister. During the trial you could see this being played out in full view of everyone in the courtroom. It was like a battle of wills with neither of them knowing what the other one was thinking or revealing. It was definitely true that their communication had been shocking, almost as if they had never even spoken before and were waiting to see what the other defendants revealed before making their case. Even though this was apparent it did not affect what evidence the witnesses and the forensic teams brought to the case. That far outweighed any argument that they presented.

He was represented by his mother and for this I rated her. I often wondered if I could play the role of a defendant's mother and even though that would mean that my son was still alive, I really couldn't see myself in that position. I think as mothers we fight for our children to the end. Whether they are right or wrong somewhere along the line we always feel that the blame comes back onto us. We question what we did right or wrong for them to end up in the situation that they find themselves in. We have babies and do the best by them, invest in them for all of their teenage years and beyond but it's still not enough for them to be examples of what society wants. You dig really deep inside yourself to try to answer all of the questions that you have to try to make sense of it, to find someone to blame ultimately for the outcome. The truth of the matter is, for me, if I continued to try to search for the answers, I would never be able to live out the life that I am supposed to live. There is a process that we have to go through in life and along the way we make choices that can change our paths for the better or the worse. What has to happen after that is quite simple. Live with the consequences. Andre had his life taken from him, there is absolutely nothing that I can do to change that outcome. Death is final. The young men that decided to take his life whether they meant to do it intentionally or not have to face the consequences of their actions. That is not final. It is for a period of time and then although time has been lost, at some stage they will be able to try and have a good life again.

The proceedings didn't take too long. The Judge delivered the outcomes of their appeals. They were rejected and that was the end of that. We left the courtroom, made our way to the very dark, stuffy family room that we had been allocated and waited for the barristers to brief me before being escorted back out to the front of the building to begin the journey home. As I stepped out of the front of the building, I could see some groups of people had congregated. They were huddled together and there was lots of raised voices and side to side animated movement. It was Fabio's family.

"Keep walking", Katy told me.

She could sense the tension that was happening in front of us the same way that I could. I kept my head straight and kept walking. I had my sister Hayley with me and all I could think was that I wanted to get to the station, on the train and back home where I could start to put this all behind me again for the third time. Just as we started to approach where the group was congregated, I could hear the screams of Fabio's mother as all of her focus turned to me.

"You fucking bitch! Fucking bitch", she screamed as she stormed across the forecourt.

Closely followed by her family who were trying to hold her back so that she could not approach me. We continued to walk away from the commotion. My head was banging. What had I done to her to warrant being called a bitch? Did she blame me for her son going to prison? Maybe she did. I couldn't believe the audacity of these parents. I think that they really believed in their hearts that their children would be let out. That was never going to happen so now they needed to face the reality that was laid in front of them just like I had to when I looked at my son laying in the mortuary. There were so many things that I needed to deal with since Andre had been killed. So much had happened in a year. People came and people went. I went from having so many people present in my life and that of the boys but once everything started to come to an end one by one everyone went back to their normal lives. I didn't know what the new normal was going to look like I just knew that I needed to keep surviving. I had met a whole new group of people, bereaved families who had gone through what I had gone through? I found it often difficult to gauge the length of time that they were living with the loss of their children. Some whom I thought were recently bereaved like me had been bereaved for a number of years and as more young people became murdered not just in Croydon where I lived but across the country, I could see those parents now following the same patterns and journey that I had been on for almost a year.

I needed to think about how I was going to start getting back to work, a career that I had worked hard for. It was going to be tough as my memory was no longer very good. I also had become involved in lots of community-based work. Trying to find solutions to knife crime. Not something that I pushed to be part of but something that found me and dragged me in. My life became about meetings and conversations. Trying to find strategies and supporting other families. Everyone wanted to hear what I had to say whether that was seated around the Borough Commanders table at Croydon Police station or talking to a group of excluded children at an event. It gave me a sense of being involved and talking about Andre meant that more and more people would know his name, his story and in turn he would not be forgotten.

Don't get me wrong, it took its toll on me. It is hard to continuously recall the trauma that you have lived through on demand. Police had me doing all sorts of things and it was these meetings which led to the planning of Andre's one year memorial and yet again the planning commenced.

CHAPTER EIGHTEEN
ONE YEAR MEMORIAL

One year came past very quickly. How had it been one whole year without my son. I had lived through all the first anniversaries, and they were all very painful. My first Christmas without him and I was a mess. I found myself slumped on the sofa intoxicated. I had many events to attend for the children, but I just couldn't get myself motivated. I was grateful for Andre's friends. Pat took the boys to her house to do Christmas activities with her family. I couldn't shake the feeling that I had. I was grateful for my niece Jadine who came and spent the night with me. She was not going to allow me to go through this by myself. Christmas day after visiting the cemetery we went to the Wine bar that Mandy worked at and had a large family dinner, all of us together. It kept me busy but as much as I tried to keep my mind on the festivities, I couldn't shake Andre from my mind. Andre loved Christmas. It didn't matter what age he got too he was always the first up in the morning exciting his siblings. He would get up so early in the morning that by dinner time he would be fast asleep in his bed. We would have to convince him to get back up and show an appearance at the dinner table. He would come back downstairs but would soon be sleeping off the food that he had eaten. Christmas was a big deal in our family, but the first Christmas without Andre had been unbearable for us all.

Next was his first birthday without him. Unintentionally I had all three of my sons in March. The month started with Amari on the fourth. The first year I had to really try hard to pull a gathering out of the bag so that his birthday was special for him. I needed to celebrate his new age and for him to not feel guilty for wanting to be happy, to celebrate and to receive gifts. Andre and Amari's birthdays were four days apart with Andre's being on the eighth. Andre stopped wanting a fuss being made once Amari was born, instead he insisted that they had a joint celebration with one cake. I would buy them one rectangular cake and put candles up each end for them to blow out. Andre adored Amari they were so close considering that there was eleven years between them. As mentioned before, Andre's first birthday without him was spent at the court with a gathering at the cemetery afterwards. Everyone who needed to be there was there.

Within two weeks it was the final March birthday for the year, Ashley's. Those two weeks were a real struggle mentally. I felt guilty for not having the motivation to organise proper celebratory gatherings for Ashley's birthday, but I found that it took me a long time to recover from missing Andre for his. It wasn't fair but I think that they understood. This is definitely an area that I need to continue working on and improve for their benefit.

The first Mother's Day, made special by the boys and Andre's friend Lilie. She helped the boys to make me a special card from Andre which had his photo in it and a message from him telling me that he was okay. All mothers' days going forward I wanted to give a miss. Andre made me a mother when he was born in 1997, the Saturday before Mother's Day. Since his passing my own mother would be lucky if she saw me on that day of the year. I had two other children, but I had nothing to celebrate or be appreciative for. The first Mothers' Day especially I felt that I should not celebrate as I had failed as a mother. I would go to the cemetery and lay flowers and the boys would try their best to cheer me up and make the day special but nothing in my life felt the same anymore.

On my first birthday without Andre, I decided that I needed to get my friends together and head out for a dance and a drink. I got dressed up in a tightly fitted blue dress which I had brought especially for the occasion. I had lost so much weight through the grief that I was now able to wear anything that I wanted, and I hadn't been in that position for a very long time. I had a really good night. I had drunk so much champagne and danced like I had not danced in years. Towards the end of the night, I became so overwhelmed and guilty for having fun that I ended up sat in the garden crying my eyes out. I was thirty-seven when Andre was killed, I was looking forward to being forty with a twenty something year old. The reality that this was never going to happen hit me like a brick. I was going to reach my milestone without him, and he was never going to see twenty. The thought alone just broke my heart. I had so many dreams and ambitions for all of us and what I was experiencing, living without him, was not one of them.

During one of my many meetings with Police I spoke about the plans that I had for Andre's one year memorial. I had decided that this was going to be an event that would involve the whole community.
I could have had it at home, but I really didn't want everyone knowing where I lived. I was still very cautious about who had access to me and my family in our new castle.

There were only a handful of Andre's friends that I allowed around me. Lilie had been there throughout, Pat and the girls and Reece. They were the only ones I trusted. Anyone who talked to Andre's old male friends from Monks Hill were not welcome. I planned to do a balloon release on Monks Hill. Not because that is where Andre was attacked, but because it was the place that he loved the most and where he had grown up. I talked through plans with them, and they decided that they would help me to make the day a success. Before the day, Police organised for one hundred blue and purple balloons to be delivered. Each balloon was to have a card attached to the bottom of it that would share a message with anyone that would go on to find it. I chose to use the lyrics out of one of Andre's tracks that he made on the card and then we listed helpline numbers for young people if they needed support in anyway.

"If you're trying to do road little man, make sure that you know your purpose", were the lyrics he shared.

Knowing your purpose became an important statement for me. I often wondered what Andre's purpose was in his short nineteen years of life. If you are religious, then you would have the belief that your life is already planned out for you to some respect. I wasn't the most religious person, but I did believe that everyone had a reason to be on earth and when they had completed whatever they came here to do they could move on. I was struggling to make sense of this and what Andre's purpose had been. The deeper I thought on the issue the more questions I seemed to have. Andre was such a humble young man. He didn't want for material things and definitely wasn't someone who became attached to belongings. He would give his trainers, coats, and clothes away to people who needed them.

Anything from school such as old textbooks that he had filled with his work, certificates of achievement or paintings he would throw them away. Birthday cards or anything that the average person would keep for emotional attachment reasons, Andre never. Now I found myself trying to make sense of this behaviour. Did Andre know that he would not need them? Is this the reason why he made no attachments to belongings whilst on earth? Friendships were also a strange thing for Andre. He had so many friendships with an array of different types of people. He was a protector of people and I loved him for that. This became more evident after he died. Maybe that was his purpose. The father of the church on Monks Hill agreed to open the church to the community so that they could light candles and say a prayer for Andre as we remembered him, one year on. I also had the CEO of a youth mentoring organisation who had worked with Andre and some other young people when he was at school contact me to have an input. He had taken Andre on his one and only visit to the Emirates Stadium to see the grounds of his beloved team Arsenal. Andre could have been a footballer himself if he had just worked at it, he was talented. I welcomed all the support that I could get on that day.

We arrived on Monks Hill and set up a gazebo on the grass where the air ambulance had landed the year previously. There were so many people gathering. I don't know how many people attended all I know is that we had one hundred balloons and not everyone could have one because we ran out. My sisters helped me to untangle and tie the purple cards to each of the balloons before we began distributing them to the attendees. I was there in body, but my mind was somewhere completely different. That day was like many of the days that I needed to get through with my head held high. That wasn't always easy. Sometimes I just wanted to drop to my knees wherever I was in front of whoever and scream out loud. I wanted to be able to let the pain out that I was feeling in the inside. It would have been like a swarm of wasps flying out of my mouth and taking all that haunted me day to day with it. Today wasn't that day. I had to pull myself together and get through it.

I stood on the pavement on the side of the road looking at the crowd of people who had congregated. All holding one of the balloons that we had provided or holding their own which they brought. I liked to stand back. From a distance you can always see what you can never see from inside the crowds. The different people that would congregate together, people you never noticed when you were up close and those who you never expected to see.

As I stood there a black jeep descended onto the estate with blacked out windows. It pulled to a halt and the occupants jumped out. It was D, his friend who I later went onto address as The Gorilla Man and another man introduced to me as Ashley. They planned to speak to the young people in the church once we had released the balloons.

"Aunty is that, Ashley Walters?", my niece asked me.

I think that I must have been on a different planet because the name meant nothing to me at that point, even though it had been previously discussed.

"Who?", I replied.

"You know, Top Boy, So Solid Crew", she said.

So Solid Crew I knew about maybe I was showing my age now. Twenty-one seconds was a hit back in my younger days. He added a stir to the gathering. The young people were buzzing by his presence. As usual there were camera crews and newspaper reporters present and the entire balloon release was aired live on Facebook by the press. There was a heavy police presence, but they remained respectful and stood back. I remained further away on the pavement as the countdown was started to release the balloons. Mandy kicked into organisation mode and led the countdown before hundreds of balloons were released into the sky. I took out my phone. I started to record as the balloons disappeared off into the sky. What was clearly blue and purple balloons vanished into the sky into tiny dots. I was back in my bubble, fixated by the sky. I stared on for a while whilst everyone else milled about on the grass.

After a while, like I had done a year ago I began to walk towards the church, and everyone followed. As I stood looking at the tiny church I watched as everyone began to file inside. There was a queue forming outside. I felt strange. Some of these young people had probably never been inside a church before or only to bury a friend and there they were going into to support their friend's family and more importantly remember the friend they loved and lost. I was people watching. There was definitely a tension in the air. Andre was so diverse in his friendship groups you could see the divide happening. Some of the boys were having their own conversations in places along the street. I was a schoolteacher and now with my new level of hypervigilance I could feel the tensions. I kept my eyes on them trying to work out whether the conversations were friendly or not. There was still a level of tension between some of them. Trust had been broken and there were still some unanswered questions about the level of involvement of people who had called themselves Andre's friends.

As I thought it, a commotion started. The police officers that were present looked at me as they drew for their radios to call for support.

"It's alright, I will deal with it", I told them as I headed towards the boys who were now in the middle of the street.

As usual they stood there looking at me with that bemused look on their faces. The last thing that I wanted was for police to fly up to the estate because of these boys' behaviour. I marched into the middle of the street and grabbed the one that was making the most noise. Honestly, as I write this, I cannot even remember clearly who the people were that were creating the commotion, but I am sure of the response that I gave. I mean seriously I am only 5ft 4 at a push and at the time wasn't holding much weight because of my grief but one thing that I was sure of was that I was able to demand respect.

"Get over here now!", I shouted to the one that was acting as the aggressor.

I dragged him across the street and onto a driveway of a house a few doors down from the church. My message was clear.

"This is not about you; I don't care what you think or feel about anyone else who is here right now. If you have a problem, then leave but don't bring any animosity or ill feeling here on this day", I ordered.

I had a way of demanding respect from young people. I was never scared of them. I don't think that I have ever met a young person that I have not been able to engage with on some level. That was my gift, it was what I was able to do easily whether in a classroom, playground, park, or on the estate. It helped that I was Andre's mum. These boys had a thing about being respectful to 'Auntie's' and I had most definitely become one of them to many young people over the years.

They had two choices. Go inside the church with everyone else who had come together to light a candle and think about the memories that they had with Andre or leave and not be a part of it. One of the boys decided to go and the other entered the church. The church was packed. There was nowhere to sit and even though I was offered a seat, I was happy to just sit on the floor of the aisle of the church and watch. The two Ashley's spoke to the young people, I had never met either of them before but they both had very powerful stories to share with all who was listening. Ashley Walters spoke about his own lived experiences, giving the young people some hope for their futures regardless of their starting place and Ashley 'Gorilla Man' spoke passionately about young people and their need to act like chimpanzees rather than striving to become Gorillas or Silverbacks. I was in ore of their wisdom and watching the young people sit quietly reflecting on the loss of their friend and listening with great depth filled me with a warm feeling of hope.

The Memorial Day was the last time that I ever really hosted such an event to remember Andre. Some of his friends stayed in contact, in particular a young man called Reece. He had known Andre from Primary school days. Both played for the same local football clubs and had formed a friendship over the years. Reece hadn't been one of the friends that was always around, but he was at the house on the odd occasion. I remember him sitting on the sofa behind the door one evening when I was getting ready to go out. I often changed outfits and shoes and paraded them in front of Andre to gage his opinion. He was brutally honest with me and if something didn't look good, he would tell me. Reece found our interactions amusing and I would catch him smiling, a smile that was infectious, ear to ear with beautiful white teeth.

In the months and years to follow, Reece's presence became more, and he became part of the family. He would turn up at the house to check on us and he was able to build a relationship with both my boys which helped them to deal with the loss of their brother.
Reece wasn't a replacement brother but another bigger brother and Ashley in particular enjoyed and valued having Reece around. There was no other friend for me who I felt truly came in and stayed in like Reece did. A week could not pass by without him popping his head over the fence. Reece was always there, Birthdays, Anniversary's, Mothers Days, Valentine's Day, and many other days in between. We talked about so many different things. Sometimes Reece would cry, his grief was so bad that he often questioned himself and what his own future would hold. He couldn't get over the loss of his friend and the entire issues surrounding the set-up notion that had been presented.

I appreciated him, I could have conversations with Reece that I couldn't have with my own children, because he understood. We relied on each other and looked out for one another. Reece held everyone accountable and made sure that they attended our anniversary BBQ's and Andre's birthdays. Reece was the plug to everyone and in those first few years of losing Andre, Reece became like an adopted son.

Getting through that first year and visiting all those first milestones without Andre was one of the hardest things to do. The years started to pass rapidly but the pain and loss never got easier.

CHAPTER NINETEEN
LIVING WITHOUT HIM AND REFLECTIONS

Regaining some form of normality and routine was important to me. For a year I had been living a life that I was unfamiliar with. There had been some highs but mainly lows. The only aspect of my life that I had left to find the inner strength to face, and challenge was returning to work. The anxiety that I had about walking back into that building was intense. It was a place that I loved, but I had real worries about how I was going to cope. Firstly, I was unsure what the response would be like. Not only being a teacher and having to face questions from colleagues and students but also for being the mother of an ex-student who many of the current staff and students knew and loved. So many memories were held inside that building. Everywhere that I went within the school conjured up a memory of my boy. There were memories from the first day that we visited that school before he joined in Year seven right up until he left in Year eleven. The school was Andre's first choice. I wanted him to sit entry exams for other schools, but he refused point blank. He was impressed with the Astro turf and other sports facilities and loved the modern feel of the space inside the building.

I had sat outside another school waiting for him to finish his entry exams after a morning of threats and promises if he didn't go, anxiously hoping that he would give it his best shot. He eventually came running out with the other students with that familiar cheeky grin on his face as if he was very proud of himself. Andre was tiny, smaller than his peers in both height and weight. He had been like that all his life. He smiled at me as he hopped into the front seat and pulled on his seat belt.

"How was the test?", I asked him, hopeful by his happy mood.

He looked at me with a cheeky smile and then replied in a very confident and proud manner.

"I didn't do it!", he said, still grinning from ear to ear.

"What do you mean you didn't do it?", I questioned with slight irritation in my voice.

"I want to go to Ashburton", Andre said. "I already told you that".

It suddenly dawned on me that I had a son who was actually too clever for his own good. Andre knew that telling me that he wasn't going to attend wasn't an option, but he also knew that if he didn't try whilst sitting the test there would be nothing that I could do about it. Refusing to answer the questions or only partially completing the test would not get him a place. As much as it infuriated me because I really wanted him to have the best chance at an education, there was nothing that I could do about it now. This is just one example of the type of personality that Andre had. No one could convince him to do things that he didn't want to do. He had a mind of his own, that I was sure about.

As I entered the school on my first day back, I could picture him running along the corridor with his plaits swinging. Certain rooms would also trigger quite painful memories for me such as my teaching classroom, a place where him and his friends would often come too during breaks and lunchtimes. The food room where I taught Andre and a group of other boys in the same year to cook as part of an alternative engagement strategy. They loved cooking, they fully enjoyed making the array of dishes that I planned for them on a weekly basis. But even more than that they enjoyed having the time together and having me in the class to facilitate their questions and talk through any issues. They felt like they had achieved something with their, 'almost edible' dishes that they created every time they left the classroom.

Nobody knew what to say to me. Whether to ask me if I was okay or just treat me like they did before my son was murdered. Those closest to me and Andre just knew how I was feeling. Andre's Head of Year whilst he was at the school along with others were also heartbroken. Sometimes as we approached each other in the corridor, there were no words to speak, but we both would pass each other with tears in our eyes. I was so grateful to have a team of friends at work who were there to help and support me to get back up in some of these darkest times.

The second greatest struggle that I had was with my memory. I underestimated the impact that the trauma of losing Andre would have on my brain. I may as well have never trained to teach because at this point of returning I could not even remember anything. I struggled to recall names of pieces of equipment that I used in the workshop. Everything became a thingamajig or a whatchamacallit. I was a good teacher and losing the ability to recall or remember information became a real struggle for me. During the exam season as I sat in the canteen collecting in students' phones and placing them in envelopes, I think it became real how much my memory was struggling to process information. These children stood in front of me were children whom I had known since Year 7. I knew all of them individually but on this day, as a colleague and I was sat there trying to carry out phone duty the reality of what I was dealing with hit me.

Students approached the desk one by one to hand in their phones.

"What's your name again?", I asked.

Each one stopped and looked at me bemused.

"Miss, you are kidding right?", they would ask.

I felt embarrassed that I couldn't remember their names and the quicker the students were appearing at the desk the harder it was getting for me to remember. I think that they thought that I was joking around but I really wasn't. The pressure that was being placed on me took its toll and my anxiety and depression was rising. Once I had finished work, I was going straight home and falling asleep on the sofa. I would wake up hours later and then felt guilty that the boys had to fend for themselves. I was falling into a darker place. Going back to work was supposed to be a step into the right direction but instead it was having a detrimental effect on my mental health.

One evening I was feeling so defeated and decided to have a few glasses of rum to calm me down. I finished the bottle, and my mood was still extremely low. I was battling with how I was feeling, and the constant feeling of loss was affecting me and my ability to function. I had started to slide backwards. The return to work and the pressure being placed on me, mixed with my grief had become too much. I found a bottle of red wine and started to drink it out of a mug, and I couldn't stop. As I sat on the sofa staring at a photo of Andre on the side, I became so overwhelmed I started crying. It was horrible, I was totally out of control. The more I sobbed the more I drank the worse my reaction to the grief became. On this night I was walking around with a black and white photo of Andre, the same one used over a year ago for his murder appeal, under my arm and the mug of red wine in my hand.

I had scared the children. They stood in the doorway watching me lose control of everything. The mother that they had watched stand tall with dignity throughout the entire ordeal was slipping further out of sight. Through their fear, they called for help from our family. All I remember is feeling as if everything that I had been through was churning up inside of me and fighting to get out. It was a pain that I had not felt before, like a fire had been relit and I was living again in the most horrendous nightmare. Things became so bad, so quickly and I ended up spread out, face down on the kitchen floor still clutching the photo in the frame of my handsome boy, vomiting and unable to find the strength to pick myself up. It was Mandy and my sister Lorraine who turned up to rescue me. Two very different characters who played very different roles in my life.

Lorraine, my sister, and I, are almost five years apart in age. Throughout everything that had happened, I felt that there were times where she would keep her distance from me. I didn't need to question it because I knew why. It was because she feels everything that I feel. Over the years we have become so in tune with each other's emotions it didn't take a lot for us both to be in floods of tears if either of us were upset. Mandy on the other hand is a very different character. Mandy takes control of situations and what she says often goes.

"I'm all dressed up, so you better get your arse up off the floor rolling around in sick", Mandy said in her normal authoritarian voice. I could tell that she was disgusted with me.

Mandy was another mother figure, someone who I relied on greatly throughout the entire time. Hearing her voice slapped me back into reality. I did get up. Together they changed my clothes, whilst mumbling about the sick in my hair and how things got to this and laid me on my side on the sofa. I could have just stayed there and sobered up but the next thing I had the paramedics taking my blood before I was carted off to the hospital for monitoring. After a few hours once the alcohol started to wear off, I discharged myself from the hospital and went back home to my children. This was a real wake up call. I had been so close to the edge on a few occasions, on my return from my second Jamaica trip with Mandy, she had called a family meeting, without me, and placed me on suicide watch. I wasn't suicidal but things were getting seriously out of control, and I finally knew that I needed to do something before I lost everything.

I couldn't speak. It felt as if I had sanded the inside of throat with the roughest sandpaper going. My eyes looked as if I had been in a boxing ring and my mood was depleted. I had been referred to SLAM for assessment which happened very quickly, and I was assessed as having severe anxiety and depression. Being told that I was depressed was scary. It was as if everything that I had been trying to hide and handle myself was now public knowledge. I needed to accept the help and I was quickly booked in for six weeks EMDR (Eye Movement Desensitisation and Reprocessing) therapy. My thoughts on the therapy and the actuality that it could possibly help made me more inquisitive to try and give it a go. I took six Tuesday afternoons off work and attended a clinic in East Croydon. The therapist explained to me the process and what each session would look like and then the work began.

"Think about the memory and hold it in your mind", the therapist said.

I had chosen three memories that were almost stuck in my brain. The funny part of this is that they were not things that I had actually witnessed with my own eyes. The first memory had been created by all the details that I had heard on the night of Andre's murder, from Police and then throughout the trial from evidence and witness statements. I had heard so much detail that it became as if I had actually, witnessed it myself. With my eyes closed I focussed on the memory that I had in my head. I could see Andre laying there on the ground again with the perpetrators standing over the top of him. I could hear him screaming in pain as they were stabbing him with the black kitchen knife and repeatedly kicking him. It took my breath away.

"Where can you feel it?", the therapist asked me.

I could feel it in my throat like a strangling pain that was stopping my natural breathing. There was a burning sensation that was raising up my neck and into my face and I could feel my eyelids flickering as I tried to hold back the tears triggered by the sound that wanted to explode out of my mouth.

"Hold the image in your head", I was instructed.

I did, and as I opened my eyes and focused on the therapist's hand, she moved her hand and fingers back and forth like a pendulum on a grandfather clock, it was the strangest experience. One that I never knew could actually be possible.

"Where can you feel it now?", she asked me.

It had moved. The pain was no longer in my throat and eyes it had moved down and was settling in my chest. She continued and after a few more minutes she stopped her movements and asked me again.

"Where can you feel it now?"

It had completely moved from my chest area, and I could feel a slight tingle in my stomach. We continued for some time until the answer that I gave her when she asked me was that it had gone.

During the next few sessions that I had with the therapist, I had the same or similar experiences. Sometimes the pain was at the front of my head, and I could feel it moving from there to the back of my neck area. When I was asked to go back and recall the memories that we had previously worked on, they were no longer so painful as the first time that I had done it. In fact, what I saw in my mind when I was recalling these memories was very different now. I knew what was happening, but I was further away, down the street and around the corner and no longer so close and affected by every action.

EMDR changed my path for the better. After the first three sessions, I was no longer getting home from work and falling asleep on the sofa due to depression. I was no longer having nightmares that kept me awake all night and I was able to remember and recall information again. I don't know where I would be if I had not been offered this therapy. I needed this level of intervention to help me to get back on track. Finally, being able to move on from those traumatic memories which had been stuck in my mind every minute of every day gave me the ability to start doing some enjoyable aspects of my life, teaching better and taking control again with confidence. For something that I couldn't even imagine working in the first place, it had actually worked wonders.

Things were still not so easy for my boys. Ashley had now left school and without any GCSE exam results he was finding it difficult to decide on what steps to take. Watching your children end up on a path that was not originally set out for them is so difficult. Both boys had dealt with the loss of their big brother in very different ways. Ashley being five years younger than Andre was able to deal with his emotions better than Amari. I believe that he was able to express how he felt emotionally whether that was anger or tears. I was able to hold him as he cried, and we could talk things through about how he was feeling. Over the past few years, I have watched him pull parts of his life back together. His passion for football and for family has come back to him. Sometimes I worry about the amount of time that he spends at the cemetery, but I know that this is part of his journey towards healing so I support him the best I can. Turning nineteen was a very difficult time for Ashley. He struggled to comprehend how his years on earth were the same as Andre's and it hit him really hard as the realisation that nineteen years is not many at all in life. Now that he has turned twenty, I have seen him become less stuck in that mentally draining state and I am hopeful that the future will be kinder to him as he settles into life and begins to live again.

Amari on the other hand has had to face some of the biggest

struggles being the youngest. So many decisions were made for him as he just watched all the tragedy unfold. For an eight-year-old he had witnessed things that most adults had not or ever will witness. Amari never cried. He had several tantrums but never spoke or showed sad emotions. He was sad, I could see it in his eyes. The sparkle that he had which I could see when looking at a photograph of him, was gone. All I could see when I looked into his eyes was sadness and heartbreak. I could manage Ashley's emotions, but Amari was completely shut down. He trusted no one and it was hard. Not only was it hard to support him to gain confidence in situations but it was also difficult to ensure that those who were caring for him at school understood his reactions, responses, and needs. All I have done is fight for what should be his right.

It wasn't long before the Primary school that he attended, gave up on him. They expressed that they couldn't manage his trauma and they did everything that they could to build a case to remove him from their school. They caused the most damage to Amari's healing process. They couldn't grasp the concept that he was unable to express emotion and often referred to him as being disrespectful for not answering their questions. After numerous sanctions, he established that by using the words yes, no and I don't know stopped him from being called disrespectful. This use of limited language remained with Amari for years. After the exclusion, which I eventually had overturned, Amari spent the finally six weeks of Primary school at another school. Year seven started off well until again the understanding for the trauma and support that he needed to learn in the classroom because of his PTSD, began to dwindle. I found myself in a very difficult situation because also working at the school which he attended I could see where the support was lacking and how the actions of some staff and their decisions were having a detrimental effect on him. Fast forward a few years, Amari is still out of school, and it breaks my heart. The simple fact that he has not even experienced school the same way that Andre did and none of what happened to our family was his fault. Amari was just an innocent child who now continues to be punished for his loss and trauma.

It is ironic and something that I often ponder over when I'm struggling to build a healthy educational experience for Amari, the schooling, and lives that the siblings of those who murdered Andre have in comparison. The way that they dealt with the situation of their siblings being arrested, charged, convicted, and put away for a long time. They seemed to cope much better with the entire situation. I know because I watched them as students in my school. Not only the siblings of those who murdered Andre but also the siblings of other murderers that I had once taught.

I will continue to fight for both of my children to have a better future. It is something that I promised to them and myself right back at the beginning of all this. I will work every hour that I can manage to ensure that they can have the things that they need and have some foundations laid for their futures. I will always push to provide for them, for them to have all the support that I was unable to give to Andre. I couldn't help him with driving lessons, a car, a holiday, clothes, shoes, or anything else that he may have needed but I have vowed that it won't be the same for Ashley and Amari. Not because I want them to be spoilt but because I feel that their starting point is much lower in comparison to their peers because of what they have had to experience and live through.

One thing that they are not short of is love. All three of my sons know that they are loved and the most important thing for me is that I can be there for them when they need me. I have faith that they will continue to heal just as I have and in time, no matter how long it takes, they will both shine again. Life for all of us has not been easy but it has definitely made us stronger. Since Andre's murder we have all had to deal with so much and sometimes I have questioned whether or not the pain and suffering will ever stop. I cannot wait for the day when the boys are out of education so that I no longer have to deal with the bureaucracy and ideology that everyone should fit into a perfect box and that if you don't fit into that expectation that it is not suitable for you so should move onto something that is life chance limiting.

One evening whilst sat at home with friends I received a call which again rocked my world. As if Deja Vu was playing out in slow motion.

"Aunty, Reece has been stabbed", I heard.

And just like before my heart shot up into my mouth. We lost Reece that night and the impact and set back that this series of events caused me, and my family was huge. I felt as if I was reliving the night of August 16th all over again. It hurt so bad that I am unable to put into words what another tragedy felt like. I guess it feels as though the pain is prolonged, starting again at the beginning. I wasn't in a good place. For the first time in a long time, I watched my boys crumble again as they dealt with loosing someone that they loved like a brother. On that night Ashley fell apart and he has been very different ever since. Amari cried, something that he had not even really done when Andre died.

This trial is not over so I cannot comment on the details of that evening, but I do know that loosing Reece is not something that I have even began to deal with yet, more than a year on. Reece played a huge part in my life, and I love him for that. He will never be forgotten and all I can pray for is that the boys are together again. It was after losing Reece that I made the decision to step back from everything that I was trying to achieve with young people to reduce knife crime. I have lost so many young people that the continuous reminders for me hurt too much. I want to try and live again. Like I said at the beginning of this book I am happy to try and do that now with a different approach. I don't want to hurt everyday but remember those that I have loved and lost along the way with a smile on my face. I have two angels looking out for me and I know that they would be happy for me to try and free myself from this burden and live out the time that I have left on earth happy.

Writing this book has given me the opportunity to reflect on my heartbreak and healing. I have revisited every event and emotion that I have felt throughout the past six years and emptied it from my heart where I have carried it for so long and onto these pages. I have freed myself from the anger that I felt for so long because carrying that forward in life can only be like self-destruction. Now I am ready to live the rest of my story and make it count.

Andre, I will love you forever son. My first love. The one who made me a mother, who taught me to love and to always fight for better. I miss you every single day of my life and will never forget what joy you brought to me.

Reece, I thank you for everything that you did for me and the boys after Andre died. Your love was felt, and you too will never be forgotten and will always be in my heart.
Until we meet again boys.

Andre Martell Aderemi
8/03/1997 – 16/08/2016

&

Reece Young
21/10/97 – 30/03/2021

IMPACT STATEMENT

Early March 1997, a month before my 18th Birthday, I gave birth to Andre Martell Aderemi. I fell in love with him as soon as he was placed in my arms. Twenty-two hours of labour and with the umbilical cord wrapped twice around his neck his entry into the world wasn't easy but I vowed to devote my life to keeping him safe and raising him the best I could.

As a young mum I knew that I had to work extra hard to battle the stereotyping and prove to the world that I could be a good parent regardless of my age. Having Andre gave me the motivation and perseverance to make my dreams a reality and together we began building a life that my boy and I were comfortable with.
Andre watched my struggles. Through college and later University training to be a teacher, he witnessed the sacrifices that I made to succeed, and I would hear him talk to his friends about how proud he was of me. These journeys together are what gave us a tight bond, I was able to include Andre in every aspect of my life and as he got older, he would talk to me openly and honestly about what was going on in his. We knew each other inside out and with him by my side anything was possible.

Andre was also an amazing big brother to Ashley (15) and Amari (9). The boys, MY 3A's together created a home that was happy and loving. They supported each other, looked out for each other, and loved each other. All three having a slumber party in the front room eating junk food and watching box sets or out together in the park on the estate competing against other residents in football matches. Ashley and Amari looked up to and adored their brother. They were proud of him……Andre the footballer and coach teaching them all the footy tricks. Andre the pancake flipper, the tuna and pasta bake maker. The water fights and play fights. The big brother discipline and love that only a big brother can give.

A normal life. Home, Marriage, Three Sons, Two dogs and a Career.

The night I heard that Andre had been stabbed I took what felt like the longest drive of my life. Arriving and seeing my son laying on the ground with his chest being opened up and not being able to touch him, to be with him after being told that he was screaming for me was the 1st time my heart broke. Knowing for the 1st time in his life I wasn't there to protect him, to make it better to hold his hand when he needed me.

Following behind the Ambulance with blue flashing lights watching the paramedics fighting with him and praying that God don't take him from me. Arriving at the hospital and having the door shut on me and left to wait for news and when the news came feeling like my life had just been snatched from me. I could have died that night with my son. I couldn't believe what I was being told and my whole life as I knew it disappeared before me.

We left our home, gave away our pets and moved 45 miles away from our family to keep everyone safe and I failed. I dropped my son to the place he was murdered, and it doesn't matter how many times I am told that it is not my fault, or I wasn't to know I will live with the guilt of not being there for him for the rest of my life.

I shut down, my marriage disintegrated, and my children broke. I went into auto pilot. Looking at My Andre through the glass at the mortuary. Staring at him, my handsome son, my baby boy, laying still with his eyes closed sleeping peacefully. I wanted to touch him, kiss him, tell him that I love him, shout at him to get up and stop playing games but I couldn't. I never ever got to see him again. Nine weeks before a funeral all the information that I had to take in and process. I chose not to process it. To not admit that it was happening to me, my family, and my son. To deal with it all as if it was a job, a task to complete, that it would all eventually be over, and I could get back to normal.

But I don't know what normal is anymore. My mum, Andre's Nanny taking anti-depressants. I've watched my mum breakdown. My mum wanted to be strong for me but could not herself deal with the death of her 1st grandson.

My eldest sister avoided me. She is broken hearted and feels the pain that I feel as though she lost a child of her own. My youngest sister who had a business on Monks Hill gave up her work. To relive the pain of what Andre felt each day of work was too much for her. Grandparents, Siblings, Aunties, Uncles, Cousins, and friends distraught and effected by the huge loss of Andre in our lives. He played a central role in our family.... the heart and soul of everything.

Every time I think about Andre's last hours it sends me over the edge. I have tried to block it out because I don't think that I will be able to cope if I accept that these things actually happened to my son. I'm scared to accept that he died a brutal death, to believe that he is never coming home and to know that I will never hear his voice, receive a big sloppy kiss, or feel his arm around my neck. I would swap places with him in a heartbeat.

If I did not have my other two boys to keep fighting for, I would just end it all. Waking up every day feeling the loss of Andre in my life. Nothing really makes any sense anymore. I don't have his room to sit in to feel comfort. I'm in a house that's not home and has no memories of my son. My passion for teaching has gone and his belongings are in boxes.

What type of life will his brothers have with a paranoid mother like me? Not wanting them to have friendships for fear of them being disloyal. Being a prisoner in the house in case one of them gets hurt. Not allowing them any freedom for fear that they make a wrong choice.

I hear people telling me that I am a strong woman, but the truth is that I am not engaging in my feelings. I'm not strong I'm just avoiding the truth to protect my heart from breaking any more than it already has. I have to battle with myself every day to get up, get on and get some stability back for my boys. I want them to stop living in fear and if I could erase the knowledge, they have of their brother's death I would.

Andre was a loving, caring, funny, clever, outgoing loyal young man that had some really special unique qualities about him. I know he loved us more than anything and I know he knew how much I loved him. He also knew that if I ever lost him that it would kill me. Andre loved life always smiling and always happy and whilst I am desperate to try and start living life and remember the special child I had I find it extremely painful to even recall how he looks or sounds because even the smallest glimpse of him brings me to tears.

Printed in Great Britain
by Amazon